*Everyday Letters
for All Occasions*

JACK MAGUIRE

Everyday Letters for All Occasions

A Roundtable Press Book

GUILDAMERICA
B O O K S ®

DOUBLEDAY BOOK & MUSIC CLUBS, INC.
Garden City, New York

Published by GuildAmerica® Books,
an imprint and a registered trademark of
Doubleday Book & Music Clubs, Inc.,
Dept. GB, 401 Franklin Avenue,
Garden City, New York 11530

ISBN: 1-56865-085-X

To Susan Meyer and Marsha Melnick,
my letter-perfect friends

Contents

Note to the Reader

THE NEED to write letters from time to time is a fact of life. *Everyday Letters for All Occasions* is designed to help you meet that need and to derive the most benefit and pleasure from doing so. Good letters can improve a personal relationship, enhance your social life, and further your personal well-being. They can also make a sale, clarify a business plan, get you a raise, or motivate your staff.

The ability to write an effective letter does not rely on a special talent. Instead, it depends on knowing the basic principles and applying them with common sense in order to achieve the particular result you want to achieve. *Everyday Letters for All Occasions* gives you practical, up-to-date advice on why, when, and how to write letters—advice that you can act on quickly and conveniently. It also offers over 200 model letters relating to a full range of different social, business, and official situations. And it provides samples of standard letter formats and the correct forms of address to use when writing people with special titles.

Everyday Letters for All Occasions enables you to say what you want and need to say in writing. By using the model letters in this book to help frame your own, you will soon learn to write with less difficulty and more confidence. Even more important, you will continue to realize more effective, interesting, and rewarding possibilities in your social, business, and official correspondence.

PART ONE

Writing an Effective Letter

ONE

When and Why to Write a Letter

WHY WRITE A LETTER when you have the option of telephoning or visiting the intended recipient?

When might writing a letter be more appropriate or more productive for your purpose than a telephone call or a personal visit?

In most situations you have to decide for yourself whether to write a letter instead of telephoning or visiting, based on the situation at hand, your personal style of communicating, and how you think the recipient might respond. You can begin by considering this issue from the opposite perspective: When is it better to telephone or visit instead of writing a letter? In general, it is better to telephone or visit in the following social or business situations:

- You do not want to create a tangible record of your message that might fall into the wrong hands or that might survive as an unpleasant reminder.
- You are on very close terms with the recipient, and the two of you are accustomed to speaking with each other rather than writing to each other.
- You need a simple answer to an easy question.
- You want to double-check that you have the correct date, time, or place of a meeting or event.
- You need to discuss or settle something as soon as possible.

- You want your communication to have a more personal, interactive tone.
- You want to make sure that a previous message has been received and understood.

Now, let's look at the other side of the issue. Here are some general guidelines regarding social or business situations where it is better to write a letter than to telephone or visit:

- *Write when you are seriously concerned about inconveniencing the other person with a telephone call or visit.*

A telephone call or a visit can be an unwelcome intrusion into someone's home life, even if you know that person's day-to-day schedule fairly well. In contrast to homes, business offices are usually more open to a telephone call or visit at any time during business hours. However, the call or visit should be relatively short and uncomplicated, since the recipient's spur-of-the-moment "response time" is likely to be fairly limited.

- *Write when you want to create a record of your communication either for yourself, for your recipient, or for both of you.*

In terms of social situations, you may want the other person to have a tangible (and potentially permanent) reminder of your invitation, thanks, congratulations, sympathy, or apology. You yourself may want to copy certain correspondence so that you'll remember what you wrote.

In the business world, many situations call for written records. Examples include making an order or reservation; registering a complaint; offering a commendation, endorsement, or reference; applying for a job or promotion; announcing an acceptance, rejection, or resignation; and conveying information that should be available for future reference.

- *Write when custom or protocol demands a letter.*

Socially, one must consider what is customary in society-at-large as well as what is customary within one's own inner circle of family and close friends. Sometimes the same custom prevails in both social realms; other times, there are important distinctions to be made.

Among the social situations in which a letter is almost always expected, no matter what the custom within one's inner circle may be, are: inviting someone to a formal dinner, event, or wedding; thanking someone for an overnight (or longer) stay; and expressing sympathy to someone whose loved one has died.

In terms of business situations, private individuals dealing with business organizations are generally expected to write their orders, reservations, complaints, references, applications, and fund-raising requests. As for employees of business organizations, they must learn and follow company protocols regarding when they are expected to write instead of telephone or visit both inside the company itself and outside the company, when they need to communicate with customers, clients, or associates.

• *Write when you are communicating a detailed body of information, and accuracy is important.*

Any social communication that involves giving times, dates, directions, or instructions is usually better made in writing. In the business world, numerous communications involve facts and figures that are more efficiently conveyed in writing than in conversation.

• *Write when you think that the other person will absorb and respond to your message better if it is written rather than spoken.*

Whether in a social or a business situation, many people get painfully embarrassed when they are the object of spoken praise, congratulations, or complaint. Therefore, writing them instead of telephoning or visiting may be kinder and more effective. It's also better to write than to speak if you want to make sure that a very busy, highly distractible, or habitually inattentive person will remember what you have to communicate.

• *Write when you want to confirm either your feelings about a recent experience with the other person or the content of a recent discussion with the other person.*

In the social world, post-party or post-overnight-stay thank-you notes fall into this category. In the business world, there are frequent occasions when a telephone call or a visit generates information that's important enough to be codified in letter or memo form.

TWO

How to Write an Effective Letter

THIS BOOK helps you to write effective letters by giving you hundreds of models of correspondence that you can use on a case-by-case basis for different kinds of social and business situations. Nevertheless, no matter what type of letter you are writing, there is a general process you can follow for making it as effective as possible.

1. Prepare before writing.

About half the time you put into writing a letter should be spent planning it *before* you write the first draft. (This planning phase includes the next two guidelines.) A letter is a singular and lasting reflection of your ability to be clear, coherent, and thoughtful. In order to avoid writing anything unintelligible, incomplete, or inappropriate that you'll regret on second thought, do your "second thinking" ahead of time.

2. Develop a clear understanding of your purpose and your reader.

The purpose of a letter is to motivate your reader to think, feel, or act in some specific way. Bear in mind that an effective letter is not necessarily one in which you say what you *want* to say. Instead, it's one in which you say what you *need* to say to achieve your desired outcome.

For example, if you're writing a letter of complaint, you may want to vent all your anger on your reader. However, this may not get you the response that you desire: sincere regret from the reader and quick, courteous action to address the complaint. Instead of expressing anger, it is better to express concern and subtly appeal to the reader's sense of justice.

If you're writing a letter of condolence, you may want to pour out all your own grief relating to the death, or you may want to dispel the gloom by being very upbeat and diverting. However, neither approach will achieve the main purpose of a condolence letter: acknowledging and comforting the recipient's feelings. It is better to gently let the reader know that you share in his or her sorrow and that you are available if needed.

To focus better on your purpose for writing, ask yourself these questions regarding the person to whom you are trying to communicate:

- What is my reader like? What other people might read my letter? What are they like?
- What does my reader know about me and the subject about which I am writing? What are my reader's attitudes toward me and that subject?
- What do I want my reader to think, feel, or do as a result of what I'm writing?
- How can I best express what I have to say so that my reader will react in the desired way? What does and doesn't my reader need to know? What style and tone should I use in the letter?

3. Organize what you have to say in the letter by making an outline.

Jot down notes on a sheet of scrap paper, so that you have an approximate step-by-step chart of what you're going to say in the letter. Keep working on this outline until you feel confident about the overall content and shape of your letter.

Effective letters tend to follow the same basic arrangement. In general, it is best to state the purpose of your letter clearly and succinctly within the first paragraph. The rest of the letter should consist of material supporting this main purpose, with each paragraph addressing a different main point in descending order of importance. The ending of your letter should not introduce new information but should offer a polite farewell, with (if appropriate) a brief restatement of your main purpose.

In your outline you can jot down specific words, phrases, and sentences that you want to include in your letter. All parts of your letter should flow smoothly together, so it also pays to think ahead about transition phrases—about the specific words, phrases, and sentences you will use to move from one part of the letter to the next.

If you don't make a copy of your final letter to keep for yourself, consider keeping your outline, rough as it may be. Put it in a correspondence file with the recipient's name and date. In the future this will enable you to recall what you have—and haven't—already told the recipient, which could help you to become a better correspondent.

4. Write your letter using language that is simple, clear, and concise, so that your reader can easily understand what you say.

One of the most common errors in letter writing is trying to impress the reader, or "formalize" the letter, by using overly sophisticated, technical, or abstract language. Here are examples of each of these three types of inappropriate language:

- *Overly sophisticated* language uses words that are more complicated than necessary to communicate the message. Compare the overly sophisticated statement "Pursuant to our conversation, I herewith enclose a document for your perusal," with the more fluid, conversational statement "In response to our conversation, I'm enclosing a report for you to read."
- *Technical* language consists of jargon and buzz words. Compare the technical, "in" character of the statement "We're green-lighted for a re-tread of the McNulty project, so that it's in sync with integrated management programming," with the simpler, more common-speech character of the statement "We've been authorized to revise the McNulty project, so that it can be more easily supervised by a greater number of managers."
- *Abstract* language is unnecessarily vague, rather than being as

direct and specific as possible. Compare the abstract statement "Your representative's conduct leaves something to be desired" with the more concrete statement "Your representative does not behave in a professional manner during service calls."

5. Rewrite your letter, editing it to make sure that it serves its purpose, is well organized, and uses language that is simple, clear, and concise.

Rewriting not only gives a letter its final polish, but also helps to ensure that it's as effective as you can make it be. If it's worth taking the time to write, it's worth taking the time to rewrite.

Begin by rereading your first draft, pretending that you're the recipient. Afterward, work on any passages that you think may be problematic for your recipient: e.g., that seem confusing, objectionable, or out of character with your relationship.

In addition, try reading your first draft out loud. This is an excellent way to check for language that sounds unnatural, impersonal, or awkward.

Here is a checklist you can follow during the process of editing and rewriting your letter:

• Is the purpose of the letter—the basic message I want to communicate—stated clearly and succinctly in the first paragraph?
• Have I done the best job that I can do to get my reader to respond in the way that I want him or her to respond?
• Is it written so that it can be easily understood by my reader?
• Does it contain everything that's important for my reader to know in order to achieve my purpose?
• Are there any unnecessary, redundant, or overly wordy parts that I could easily eliminate?
• Is all the information accurate?

PART TWO

Types of Social Correspondence

THREE

Invitations and Acknowledgments for Dinners, Parties, and Events

THE DIFFERENCE between a formal gathering and an informal gathering is primarily a matter of appearances. A formal gathering is one involving formal dress (dinner jackets and evening gowns or cocktail dresses), formal manners, and formal invitations and acknowledgments. Generally speaking, it is a relatively large gathering, often in honor of an individual, couple, or group, such as an anniversary dinner, a celebration banquet, a welcoming party, or a wedding reception (see Chapter 4 for weddings). The formal tone of the occasion is set by the invitation, and it is confirmed and agreed to by the acknowledgment.

An informal gathering is a smaller, more intimate event, involving people who are relatively more familiar with each other; it is therefore more casual. Because the concept of an informal party is open to so many more interpretations than the concept of a formal party, the invitation bears even more responsibility to set the right tone.

Given this situation, most people, ironically, discover that formal invitations and acknowledgments are easier to compose than their informal counterparts. The latter demand more personal creativity, while the former simply require following prescribed rules.

Let's look first at formal invitations and acknowledgments. Then we'll review informal invitations and acknowledgments.

FORMAL GATHERINGS

Offered below are the major rules that apply to formal invitations. They are followed by specific examples of formal invitations, representing the limited range of formats that are considered socially correct.

GUIDELINES FOR FORMAL INVITATIONS

- The invitations should be either engraved or handwritten on doubled sheets of high-quality white paper. They should not be printed by an offset process. If the invitations are handwritten, the wording, spacing, and layout should be the same as if they were engraved. Engraved invitations may feature one blank space within which the specific name(s) of the invitee(s) can be handwritten, or they may feature several blank spaces—for handwriting the specific names, the nature of the event, the time, and the date (see the example later in this section).
- Formal invitations should be sent at least three weeks prior to the occasion. Otherwise, an informal invitation or a telephone call, accounting for the relatively short notice, is advisable (see "Informal Gatherings" below).
- All invited parties should be mentioned by name, either on the invitation envelope (in the case of a fully engraved invitation) or on the invitation itself (in the case of a handwritten invitation). Each name should have a title (e.g., "Mr.," "Ms.," "Miss," or "Dr."). When inviting adult children of a couple, each adult child should receive a separate invitation.
- Except for titles like "Mr.," "Mrs.," and "Jr.," and if desired, the abbreviation "R.s.v.p." ("Répondez s'il vous plaît," or "Please reply"), never use abbreviations or initials in a formal invitation. Spell out all words in dates and addresses. In the case of a middle initial in a name, either spell out the middle name or omit the initial. To indicate a.m. or p.m. (if necessary), use the phrase "in the morning" or "in the evening."

- For a dinner, party, or event, always use the phrase "request the pleasure of your company," never "request the honor of your presence." The latter expression is reserved for wedding invitations.
- Write out all numbers if they are short (as a general rule, any number that is less than 100). Otherwise, use numerals. Telephone numbers are never used in formal invitations. If the invitation asks for a response ("Please reply" or "R.s.v.p.," with or without the phrase "Regrets only"), it should give an address for reply, not a telephone number.
- If your invitation is accompanied by an engraved "response card" for a reply (see the example later in this section), the response card should be enclosed within a stamped, self-addressed envelope. Response cards are frequently used if the gathering is being held somewhere other than the host's home, especially if it's being held at another private residence, or if the reply is to be sent to a person whose name is not specified in the invitation.

EXAMPLES OF FORMAL INVITATIONS

For a dinner at writer's home (completely engraved version):

Mr. and Mrs. Michael Brown
request the pleasure of your company
at dinner
on Friday, June the nineteenth
at eight o'clock
Twelve Henly Road
Chelsea, New York 12512

Please reply

For dinner at writer's home (partially engraved or handwritten version):

Mr. and Mrs. Michael Brown
request the pleasure of
<u>Dr. and Mrs. Abraham Liebermann's</u>[*]
company <u>at dinner</u>
on <u>Friday, June the nineteenth</u>
at <u>eight o'clock</u>
Twelve Henley Road
Chelsea, New York 12512

Please reply

---

* The underlined parts of this example may be handwritten on a partially engraved "stock" invitation, i.e., an invitation drawn from a stock of invitations that the hosts use whenever they have a dinner party at home. If invitations are engraved especially for this occasion, and if the host couple prefers to use specific names rather than the phrase "your company," only the space for the name(s) of the recipient(s) should be left blank.

For a luncheon in honor of a visiting friend or notable person at a well-known hotel (no address indication necessary):

Mr. Kevin Harleigh
requests the pleasure of your company
at a luncheon
to meet Mr. and Mrs. Lane Buttry
Saturday, November the sixth
at half past one o'clock
The Leveque Hotel

R.s.v.p.
1440 Grandview Avenue
Miami, Florida 33133

*For a special event hosted by a couple with different last names and
taking place at a restaurant for which the recipients may need an address:*

Mr. Donald Everett Youngman
and
Ms. Sara Berkley Werner
request the pleasure of your company
at a reception
on the Tenth Anniversary of their marriage
Thursday, August the twenty-first
from five until eight o'clock
The Atrium
240 Main Street
Cleveland

R.s.v.p.
Regrets only
Thirty-four Rockridge Avenue
Cleveland, Ohio 44145

For a son's birthday:

In honor of the
Twenty-first Birthday of
Bradley Hartwell
his parents
Mr. and Mrs. Ernest Jerome Hartwell
request the pleasure of your company
at a dinner dance
on Saturday, February the third
at seven o'clock
Hotel Chevalier

Please reply
1290 Ridgeley Terrace
Arlington, Texas 76016

For a couple's anniversary dinner, hosted by their children; accompanied by a reply card:

In honor of the
Fiftieth Wedding Anniversary of
Mr. and Mrs. Lawrence Fox
their son and daughters
request the pleasure of your company
at dinner
on Sunday, September the seventeenth
at seven o'clock
The Wiltshire Inn
41 Kingstown Street
Marble Heights, Vermont

Engraved reply card enclosed in separate self-addressed and stamped envelope (card can also be entirely handwritten):

[Hand-write name(s) of recipient(s)]
_____accepts
_____regrets
for Sunday, September the seventeenth

For a debutante dance, to recipient and escort/guest:

Mr. and Mrs.
request the company of
Miss Alexis Koeppel and escort[*]
at a dance
in honor of their daughter
Heather Marie Belton
on Saturday, May the twentieth
at eight o'clock
The Devonshire Club

R.s.v.p.
Seventeen Remsen Street
Seattle, Washington 98115

FORMAL ACKNOWLEDGMENTS

When writing by hand to acknowledge a formal invitation with your acceptance or regrets, you should duplicate as closely as possible the language and format of the invitation. Also use a similar quality of stationery. You should state clearly whether you are attending or not, without equivocating, and your response should be sent within several days after receiving the invitation.

When accepting, you should restate the occasion, date, time, and place exactly. When extending regrets, you have to state only the date, not the time and place. You also don't have to give the reason why you can't attend, although it is considered courteous to do so.

If only one person in an invited couple is able to attend, the invitation should nevertheless be turned down by the couple. In this situation the invited couple may want to offer a reason in their acknowledgment for extending regrets, thereby leaving it up to the host to decide whether to reissue the invitation to the individual who might be able to attend (see example below).

* The wording for a male guest would be: "Mr. Alexander Koeppel and guest."

Here are sample acceptances and regrets written in response to the formal invitations that appear above:

Acceptance to Mr. and Mrs. Michael Brown:

Dr. and Mrs. Abraham Liebermann
accept with pleasure
Mr. and Mrs. Michael Brown's
invitation for dinner
on Friday, June the nineteenth
at eight o'clock
Twelve Henley Road

Regrets to Kevin Harleigh:

Janis Kirby
regrets that a previous engagement
prevents her accepting
Kevin Harleigh's
invitation for a dinner
to meet Mr. and Mrs. Lane Buttry
on Saturday, November the sixth

Regrets to Mr. Donald Everett Youngman and Ms. Sara Berkley Werner because one person in the invited couple can't accept:

Owing to Mr. Sylvester's
absence from town,
Mrs. John Sylvester
regrets that she is unable to accept
the invitation of
Mr. Donald Everett Youngman
and
Ms. Sara Berkley Werner
for a reception
on the Tenth Anniversary of their marriage
on Thursday, August the twenty-first

Regrets to Mr. and Mrs. Ernest Jerome Hartwell:

Mr. David DiBennedetto
regrets that he is unable to accept
Mr. and Mrs. Ernest Jerome Hartwell's
invitation for a dinner dance
in honor of the
Twenty-first Birthday of
their son
Bradley Hartwell
on Saturday, February the third
because he will be traveling

Acceptance to the son and daughters of Mr. and Mrs. Lawrence Fox:

Mr. and Mrs. Morgan Thompson
accept with pleasure
the invitation of
the son and daughters of
Mr. and Mrs. Lawrence Fox
for dinner
in honor of their parents'
Fiftieth Wedding Anniversary
on Sunday, September the seventeenth
at seven o'clock
The Wiltshire Inn
41 Kingstown Street
Marble Heights, Vermont

Acceptance to Mr. and Mrs. Anthony Belton:

Miss Alexis Koeppel
and her escort
Mr. James Goodrich[*]
accept with pleasure
the invitation of
Mr. and Mrs. Anthony Belton
to a dance
in honor of their daughter
Heather Marie Belton
on Saturday, May the twentieth
at eight o'clock
The Devonshire Club

* If the escort is not yet known, or if the recipient desires, the phrase "and her escort" can be used without a proper name. For a male recipient, the phrase would be "and his guest," with or without a specific name.

CANCELING OR POSTPONING FORMAL INVITATIONS

When you have to cancel or postpone a dinner, party, or event to which you have issued formal invitations, you should send a formal handwritten note to everyone who received an invitation. The tone remains equally formal but invitation-style spacing is not appropriate.

In this note you should briefly state the reason why the invitation is being withdrawn or postponed. If you've already scheduled the new date and time for a postponed gathering, you can use this note as a reinvitation by stating the new time and date and adding "R.s.v.p." or "Please reply."

Here are some examples of formal cancellation and postponement notes:

Mr. and Mrs. Michael Brown regret that it is necessary to cancel their invitation to dinner on Friday, June the nineteenth, due to extensive damage done to their home in the recent storm.

Mr. Kevin Harleigh wishes to announce that the luncheon planned for Saturday, November the sixth, must be postponed until Saturday, November the thirteenth, at one o'clock, the Leveque Hotel, owing to an unexpected change in the travel plans of the guests of honor, Mr. and Mrs. Lane Buttry.

R.s.v.p.
1440 Grandview Avenue
Miami, Florida 33133

Because of a death in the family, Mr. Donald Everett Youngman and Ms. Sara Berkley Werner regret that they must cancel their reception on Thursday, August the twenty-first.

Mr. and Mrs. Ernest Jerome Hartwell wish to announce that the dinner dance scheduled for their son on Saturday, February the third must be postponed until Saturday, February the seventeenth, at seven-thirty o'clock, the Hotel Chevalier.

Please reply
1290 Ridgeley Terrace
Arlington, Texas 76016

CANCELING A FORMAL ACCEPTANCE

If you find that you are unable to attend a formal gathering after you have already written your acceptance note, you are obliged to write a formal note to your host as promptly as possible. If the gathering is less than a week away, a telephone call or telegram is acceptable. Unfortunately, it doesn't work the other way around: Once you have sent your regrets to a host, you can't take them back.

Your cancellation note should be written in a formal first-person-letter style. Traditionally, the note is written by the wife of the guest couple to the wife of the host couple. Briefly state the reason why you can't accept and express your apologies.

Here are examples of notes canceling a formal acceptance:

Dear Mrs. Brown,

Unfortunately, Dr. Abraham Liebermann and I will be unable to attend your dinner on Friday, June 19th, as we had originally planned. Dr. Liebermann's mother is seriously ill, and we are leaving Tuesday for Los Angeles to be with her.

We are both very sorry to have to break our engagement. Please accept our apologies.

Sincerely yours,
ROSE LIEBERMANN

Dear Mr. Harleigh,

An unexpected change in my business schedule makes it impossible for me to attend your luncheon next Saturday. I regret this deeply, as I was very much looking forward to the event and to the opportunity of meeting Mr. and Mrs. Buttry.

I hope you will understand and forgive this late notice.

Very truly yours,
ELIZABETH SMOOTS

INFORMAL GATHERINGS

An informal invitation to a dinner, party, or event is written in the same comfortable style and tone that you would use to write an informal letter. Just be careful not to turn the invitation into an actual letter! The note should be devoted totally to the purpose of inviting the recipient to your gathering. Offered below are some additional suggestions.

GUIDELINES FOR INFORMAL INVITATIONS

- In the context of written invitations, "informal" doesn't exactly mean "casual" or even "personal." To ensure good taste, avoid using preprinted invitations, colored paper, or a jocular, intimate style of writing. Instead, use high-quality letter-size plain white paper and a style that is simple and direct.
- Traditionally, invitations are extended from the wife of the host couple to the wife of the guest couple, with specific reference given to their respective husbands in the body of the letter (e.g., "Bob and I would like you and Nick to come to our party."). It isn't necessary to follow this tradition in informal correspondence, depending on how socially conservative your recipient is, but only one person should sign the invitation.
- Traditionally, in this type of correspondence, numbers under 10 and all time designations should be spelled out.
- Make sure that your invitation offers all the information that your recipient needs—the precise date, time, and place (if other than your home), without any room for error. If the gathering has a special theme, characteristic, or purpose (e.g., if it's meant to celebrate a homecoming, or if it's an outdoor party), this should be mentioned, so that your guest knows better what to expect.
- Informal invitations can and should ask for a reply in the body of the letter, rather than use "R.s.v.p." or "Please reply" outside the body of the letter.
- Informal invitations should be mailed at least two weeks prior to a gathering.

EXAMPLES OF INFORMAL INVITATIONS

Dear Lucy,

Trent and I are planning a dinner party on Saturday, June 14, at seven-thirty o'clock. We'd very much like to have you and Orrin come. Such a long time has passed since we've all been together! Please let us know if you'll be able to join us.

Affectionately,
BARBARA

———

Dear Jill and Matthew,

I've decided to inaugurate my new dining room by having some of my closest friends over to dinner. Naturally, I want you to be there! It's on Friday, April 22, at eight o'clock.

I look forward to hearing that you can come.

Love,
GINA

———

Dear Rebekah and Wesley,

Joe and I would like to invite you to a cocktail party we are hosting on Wednesday, October 10, from five to six o'clock, at the West Side Cafe, 1518 Second Avenue. It's to welcome two dear friends of ours, Howard and Una Tyler, who are visiting here from Sydney, Australia.

I know that you'll enjoy meeting each other, so please say that you can come.

Sincerely,
CASSIE

———

Dear Michelle and Evan,

Finally, summer seems to be here to stay for a while. Jim and I would like to invite you to our first outdoor party of the season on Saturday, June 30, beginning with cocktails at five o'clock, followed by dinner at seven o'clock.

We're counting on a "yes" answer from you!

Yours,
SYBIL

INFORMAL ACKNOWLEDGMENTS

The polite way of responding to an informal written invitation is to write a very brief note of acknowledgment using the same tone. This should be done as soon as possible after receiving the invitation. It is becoming more and more common for recipients of informal written invitations to telephone their acknowledgments, but properly speaking, this is not advisable unless the invitation includes the telephone number for replying or unless the gathering is less than a week away.

Your acknowledgment note should state clearly whether you'll be there or not. It should also repeat the date, time, and (if appropriate) the place. If you are sending your regrets, you should offer a brief explanation of why you can't come. If one person in the invited couple cannot come, regrets should be offered along with a brief explanation of the situation, leaving the hosts free to reissue the invitation to the person who can come if it suits their plans.

Here are some examples of notes acknowledging the informal invitations that appear above:

Dear Barbara,

I would love to come to the dinner party that you and Trent are having on Saturday, June 14, at seven-thirty o'clock. Thank you for inviting me. It has, indeed, been a long time since we've seen each other!

Your friend,
LUCY

———

Dear Gina,

Congratulations on your new dining room! I am very honored that you invited Matthew and me to help you break it in on Friday, April 22, but much to my sorrow, we won't be able to be there. We are already obligated to help supervise the Cancer Aid Benefit in Glenhaven that evening.

Please forgive our absence, and accept our best wishes for a hearty inaugural event.

Love,
JILL

Regrets because one person in the invited couple can't accept (leaving the host free to reissue the invitation to the other person):

Dear Cassie,

Thank you for inviting us to your cocktail party on Wednesday, October 10. I regret to say that Wes will be away from the city on a business trip that week, so we won't be able to come.

We're very sorry to miss the opportunity of meeting your friends from Australia. Please accept our apologies.

Sincerely,
REBEKAH

Acceptance of invitation if granted permission to be late (appropriate only if the arrival time appears to be flexible):

Dear Sybil,

Evan and I would be delighted to come to the cocktail and dinner party that you and Jim are planning on Saturday, June 30, but we have a previous engagement until six o'clock. Would it be all right to come then, instead of five o'clock?

Please give us a call to let us know (123-4567).

Cordially,
MICHELLE

FOUR

Wedding Invitations, Announcements, and Acknowledgments

UNTIL RECENTLY, wedding invitations, announcements, and acknowledgments were almost invariably formal in nature. Now, although formal correspondence is still used in the majority of cases, the steady increase of more informal lifestyles and wedding ceremonies has inspired more informal styles of invitations, announcements, and acknowledgments.

Let's start by looking at the formal styles, and then review the informal styles.

FORMAL WEDDING CORRESPONDENCE

The rules applying to conventional wedding invitations, announcements, and acknowledgments are fairly strict and widely followed. They also differ slightly from the rules applying to other, non-wedding-related kinds of formal correspondence (see chapter 3).

Guidelines for Formal Invitations

Here are the major rules pertaining to formal wedding invitations:

- The invitation is customarily engraved on the top half of a piece of high-quality plain white paper that has been folded in half. The most formal approach is then to cover the engraved surface with a piece of protective tissue, insert the invitation into an "inside" envelope (no seal) bearing the handwritten name(s) of the recipient(s), and finally, insert this inside envelope into the mailing envelope. It is perfectly acceptable, however, to eliminate the inner envelope and/or the tissue paper.

- The invitation always bears the phrase "requests the honour of" (not "honor," but the old-style "hono<u>u</u>r").

- Titles (e.g., "Dr.," "Mr.," "Mrs.," or "Jr.") are used for all names except for the name of the bride, and they are customarily abbreviated. Do not use initials in names: either spell out the name represented by the initial, or omit it altogether. Usually, the bride's middle name is not used, although it is acceptable to use it if desired.

- The words in all dates and addresses are spelled out, rather than abbreviated. For times, the phrase "o'clock" is used, never "a.m." or "p.m." If you feel clarification is needed, add "morning," "afternoon," or "evening" to the name of the day (e.g., "Friday evening"). All numbers under 100 are spelled out.

- The street address for a church or temple is not given unless the church or temple is in a big city, in which case it may be difficult for some guests to locate.

- If the wedding is taking place in a private home, or if the wedding invitation includes an invitation to the reception, then the invitation should say "Please reply" or "R.s.v.p." (which stands for "Répondez s'il vous plaît," French for "Please reply"). An alternative is to enclose a "response card" with the invitation (see the example below). In any other situation, the invitation should *not* say "R.s.v.p." or "Please reply," or include a response card.

- Instead of issuing one invitation for both the wedding and the reception, you can issue a separate invitation for the reception. To invite guests to both, you enclose an engraved "reception card" with the wedding invitation. To invite guests to the reception only, you use an engraved "reception invitation." (See below for examples of a reception card and a reception invitation.)

Generally speaking, it is not considered polite to invite guests to the reception and *not* to the wedding unless the wedding is very small and private. In the latter case, informal wedding invitations, rather than formal ones, are appropriate, while the reception invitation should be formal.

- Preferably, wedding invitations should be sent out at least six weeks prior to the wedding, but they are still acceptable as late as three weeks before. Inviting someone less than three weeks before the wedding requires a more informal note or letter that not only extends the invitation, but also apologizes and accounts for the short notice.

EXAMPLES OF FORMAL INVITATIONS

Here are examples of formal wedding invitations that apply to a variety of different situations:

Standard model:

Mr. and Mrs. Eugene Wagoner
request the honour of your presence
at the marriage of their daughter
Amy
to
Mr. Darrin Green
on Saturday, May the twentieth
at half after two o'clock
Christ Episcopal Church
Newton, Massachusetts

Divorced parents, mother remarried:

Mrs. David Rabinowitz [*]
and
Mr. Joshua Green
request the honour of your presence
at the marriage of their daughter
Rachel

to

Lewis Daniel Altschuler
on Sunday, August the twenty-first
at three o'clock
Temple Israel
238 Second Avenue
New York City

* If the mother had not remarried and had kept her former husband's last name, she would be Mrs. Ruth Green on this invitation.

Father dead, mother remarried, wedding at the home of mother and stepfather:

Mr. and Mrs. Stephen Caldwell Brinkley
request the honour of your presence
at the marriage of Mrs. Brinkley's daughter
Stella Bourne
to
Mr. Lloyd Beckford Filer
on Saturday, June the seventh
at five o'clock
Twelve Carmine Street
Albany, New York 12207

R.s.v.p.

Groom's parents giving wedding:

> Mr. and Mrs. Casey O'Malley Jervis
> request the honour of your presence
> at the marriage of
> Miss Marjorie Tilden[*]
> to
> their son
> Casey O'Malley Jervis, Jr.
> on Saturday, April the ninth
> at half after six o'clock
> Mint Valley Church
> Huntington, Alabama

* Note that this situation, unlike most others, requires the use of the title "Miss" for the bride and the absence of the title "Mr." for the groom.

Both bride's parents (the Stockleys) and groom's parents (the Judsons) giving wedding and reception:

Dr. and Mrs. William Ralph Stockley
and
Mr. and Mrs. Edward Judson
request the honour of your presence
at the marriage of their children
Veronica and Edward
on Sunday, June the seventh
at one o'clock
St. Agatha's Church
Rosendale, California
and afterward at
The King and Queen
341 Hamilton Road
Tarrington, California

R.s.v.p.
Mrs. William Ralph Stockley
Ten Camelot Place
New Britain, California 94003

Bride's unmarried uncle (mother's brother) giving wedding, reception at same church as ceremony, response card enclosed:

Mr. Milton Davis Reilly
requests the honour of your presence
at the marriage of his niece
Susan Adams
to
Maxwell Westin LaMonte
Friday, September the twelfth
at twelve o'clock
First Community Church
Verona, Florida
and afterward at the reception
in the church hall

Response card (applying to reception):

[handwritten name(s) of recipient(s)]
_____accepts
_____regrets
for Friday, September the twelfth

Bride and groom giving own wedding, at friend's home:

The honour of your presence
is requested
at the marriage of
Miss Frances Healey Conners[*]
to
Mr. Wallace Beck Felton
on Friday, April the eighth
at six o'clock
at the home of Mr. and Mrs. Adam Cushings
2221 Gloucester Avenue
Philadelphia, Pennsylvania 19123

Please reply
Mrs. Adam Cushings

* Note the use of "Miss" in this situation as opposed to most others. In the case of a bride who is divorced or widowed, the title and name is the same as the bride is currently using.

Parents of previously married bride giving wedding and reception, reception card enclosed:

Mr. and Mrs. Augustus Durwood
request the honour of your presence
at the marriage of their daughter
Gail Durwood Shelton
to
Mr. Jack Eddington Farleigh
on Sunday, July the seventh
at five o'clock
United Baptist Church
Harley, Virginia

Reception card:

Reception
immediately following the ceremony
Black Forest Restaurant
Harley, Virginia

R.s.v.p.
Twenty-seven Hillsdale Avenue
Harley, Virginia 23825

Reception invitation (can also be sent with wedding invitation, if reception is given by different person or people):

Mr. and Mrs. Grant Beverleigh
request the pleasure of your company
at the wedding reception of
their daughter
June[*]
and
Mr. John Philip Perkins
on Sunday, January the fifteenth
at six o'clock
415 Holstein Road
Niles, Mississippi 38971

R.s.v.p.

FORMAL POSTPONEMENT

If serious circumstances arise that warrant postponement of the wedding after the invitations have been engraved but before they have been sent, then the same invitations can still be sent after the new date is chosen. Simply insert a small printed card saying, "The date of the wedding has been changed from [date on invitation] to [new date]."

If the need for postponement arises after the invitations have already been sent out, and there is still time for formal notification (i.e., the notifications can be mailed at least three weeks before the

* If the reception had been given by friends of the bride, the phrase "their daughter" would have been omitted and this name would have been Miss June Beverleigh.

date on the invitation), then the most socially correct thing to do is to send out formal engraved postponement notes. In these notes, the general reason for the postponement should be stated. If the new date is already set, then the postponement note can be used as a reinvitation (see the example below).

If the wedding must be postponed and there is no time to send out formal postponement notes, then an informal note should be sent to each guest, stating the general reason for the postponement. This is also an alternative to sending out formal postponement notes, although not as socially correct.

Here are models of formal postponement notes applying to different situations:

Basic model:

Mr. and Mrs. Howard Lancaster Newsome
regret that
owing to a death in the family
the marriage of their daughter
Mary
to
Capt. Emilio Olivera
United States Army[*]
must be postponed indefinitely

---

* In the case of a military title, the name of the service should be given directly below the proper name.

If the new date is already set:

Due to Capt. Olivera's recent appointment
to the United States Army's Somalia Inspection Team
Mr. and Mrs. Howard Lancaster Newsome
wish to announce
that the marriage of their daughter
Mary
to
Capt. Emilio Olivera
has been postponed
from Sunday, January the eleventh
to Saturday, February the twenty-second
at five o'clock
Our Lady of Lourdes Church
Pocatello, Idaho
with the reception afterward
Mount Victory Lodge
Pocatello, Idaho

R.s.v.p.
1356 Nez Perce Boulevard
Pocatello, Idaho 83202

FORMAL ANNOUNCEMENTS

Formal wedding announcements let the recipients know that the wedding has already taken place, so they are never mailed before the wedding. Customarily, they are mailed the day after the wedding. They can be sent out to everyone in the couple's circle of relatives and friends who did not receive a wedding invitation, or in the event that the ceremony was very private and did not feature invitations, to everyone who was not present at the ceremony. They are never sent to someone who previously received an invitation.

The basic style of the formal wedding announcement is exactly the same as the basic style of the formal wedding invitation, except for minor changes in the wording:

- Traditionally, the announcement is always made by the bride's parents or by whoever is acting in their place. However, it is also acceptable for the bride's and the groom's parents to make the announcement jointly. In the event of a second (or later) marriage, or any situation in which the bride and groom are acting without parental involvement, the bride and the groom should make the announcement themselves.
- The year of the wedding date is always expressed and is spelled out in full.
- It is optional to express the exact place of the ceremony, other than the city. Generally, the place is expressed only if it was a church or a temple.

Here are examples of each of these types of announcements:

By bride's parents, not a religious ceremony:

Mr. and Mrs. Roger Marks Colby
have the honour of
announcing the marriage of their daughter
Terri
to
Mr. Yancy Allen Deevers
Thursday, July the first
One thousand nine hundred and ninety-three
Minneapolis, Minnesota

By bride's and groom's parents, a religious ceremony:

Mr. and Mrs. Luis Alvarez
and
Mr. and Mrs. Jorje Carlos Santana
announce the marriage of
Maria Dolores Alvarez
and
Jorje Carlos Santana, Jr.
Tuesday, May the twenty-fifth
One thousand nine hundred and ninety-three
St. Augustine's Church
Houston, Texas

By bride and groom:

Ms. Mary Gay Porter
and
Mr. Myron Samuel Schultz
announce their marriage
on Sunday, March the twenty-first
One thousand nine hundred and ninety-three
Portland, Oregon

FORMAL ACKNOWLEDGMENTS

It is not appropriate to acknowledge a wedding invitation unless it includes an invitation to a reception. The exception would be a wedding invitation that states "Please reply" or "R.s.v.p." A reception invitation should always be acknowledged.

An acknowledgment of a formal invitation should be equally formal. Use high-quality plain white stationery (as close as possible to the type of stationery used in the invitation), and in handwriting with black ink, imitate the language, arrangement, and spacing of the invitation.

When accepting, repeat only the date and time given on the invitation. It is not customary to repeat the place or the nature of the occasion. When extending your regrets, you need to repeat only the date. It is unnecessary to offer a reason for not accepting.

It is not customary to acknowledge a formal wedding announcement. If you wish to do so, then send an informal note to the bride or groom, depending on whom you know better, or if desired, to both of them (see chapter 6).

If you want to give the bride and groom a wedding present, send or deliver it *independently* of any invitation acknowledgment. When acknowledging a wedding announcement, an accompanying gift is acceptable, although not customary. (If you choose to write a note to accompany your wedding gift, see chapter 6 for examples.)

Here are examples of a formal acceptance and a formal regret:

Formal acceptance:

Mr. and Mrs. Andrew Kosiosko
accept with pleasure
Mr. and Mrs. O'Rourke's
kind invitation for
Thursday, June the sixteenth
at six o'clock

Formal regret:

Mr. and Mrs. Andrew Kosiosko
regret that they are unable to accept
Mr. and Mrs. O'Rourke's
kind invitation for
Thursday, June the sixteenth
at six o'clock

INFORMAL WEDDING CORRESPONDENCE

Many people find that formal wedding invitations and announcements do not suit their personal style or the nature of the wedding ceremony they have in mind. In this situation—and in *any* situation where the wedding is relatively small—an informal invitation or announcement is warranted, and the corresponding acknowledgment should be informal as well.

GUIDELINES FOR INFORMAL INVITATIONS

The range of appropriate formats and language in an informal wedding invitation is very broad, but here are some general guidelines to follow no matter what format or language you use:

- The invitation should be engraved or handwritten, rather than printed by an offset process, on high-quality paper. If handwritten, it is customary for the bride to do the writing. However, if note-style (rather than announcement-style) invitations are used, the groom may write to people whom he knows much better than the bride does. A member of the bride's or the groom's family may write a note-style invitation to an intimate friend who is not acquainted with the bride or groom.
- It should be clear from the envelope or the invitation itself exactly who is invited. Adult children should receive their own individual invitations.
- The date, time, and place of the ceremony (or the reception) should be clearly stated, without room for misinterpretation.
- The invitation should not serve any purpose other than conveying information and, if desired, brief sentiments directly relating to the wedding. In other words, the invitation should not be part of a larger letter. Generally speaking, the most appropriate invitations are very concise.
- It is not considered polite to ask for a reply if the invitation is just to attend a wedding ceremony, and not a reception, unless the ceremony is to be held in a private home.
- It is customary to send informal invitations at least two weeks in

advance. Any invitation involving shorter notice should be made by telephone, telegram, or personal contact.

EXAMPLES OF INFORMAL INVITATIONS

Here are examples of different types of informal wedding invitations:

Variation of a formal invitation, from both sets of parents:

Eve and Geoffrey Bridges

and

Sonya and Rolfe Hunt

invite you to share their happiness

at the marriage of their children

Catherine Anne Bridges

and

Derrick Sherwood Hunt

on Saturday, December the eleventh

at four o'clock

Trinity Presbyterian Church

Springfield, Kansas

Variation of a formal invitation, from bride and groom only, at friends' home:

Janet Lane Carter and Michael Arthur Shelton
invite you to celebrate their marriage
Friday, August the twentieth
at half after five o'clock
at the home of Virginia and Edgar Cotter
1639 Tremont Avenue
Denver, Colorado 80521

R.s.v.p.
Virginia Cotter

Note-style invitation, written by bride to acquaintances:

Dear Mr. and Mrs. Keith Hamilton,
    Douglas Riley and I are being married at four o'clock on Saturday, May the fifteenth. The ceremony is being held at the Main Street Methodist Church in Glen Valley. We would be very pleased if you could join us.

Sincerely,
VALERIE HESSEL

Note-style invitation, written by groom to good friends who know the bride:

Dear Jane and Jerry,

I am happy to let you know that Marilyn and I will be exchanging marriage vows at seven o'clock on Sunday, November the seventh. The ceremony will take place at the home of Marilyn's mother and father, Helen and Jonathan Lockesley, 1818 Riverview Road, Palomar, Arizona 13135 (map enclosed).

We both hope that you can be with us at the ceremony and at the reception afterward at the Bellingham Arms in Palomar. Please reply to Mrs. Lockesley.

Our very best wishes to you.

Love,
MARK

Note-style invitation, written by bride's mother to intimate friends:

Dear Shirley and Ed,

My daughter Jeanne will be married to Chad Solis at five o'clock on Saturday, September the twenty-fifth. The ceremony will be held at the Mt. Zion Church in Friendship, Ohio. Jeanne and Chad have asked me to invite you on their behalf.

Frank joins me in hoping that you can be with us there and at the reception afterward in the church hall.

As always,
ELAINE

INFORMAL ANNOUNCEMENTS

Informal weddings announcements take virtually the same form as informal invitations. They should always be sent *after* the ceremony, as soon as possible, and can be sent to anyone who did not receive a wedding invitation.

Informal announcements come in two basic styles: traditional announcement style, which can be either engraved or handwritten, and note style, which is always handwritten, customarily by the bride, and very brief. Informal wedding announcements should not be printed by an offset process.

Although informal wedding announcements do not need to specify the time or specific location of the ceremony (other than the city), they should specify the full date, including the year. The names of the bride and the groom should be expressed as they were known *before* the marriage. In a note-style invitation, special attention can be drawn, if desired, to how the bride now prefers to be addressed (see examples below).

Here are examples of different types of informal wedding announcements, based on the informal invitations that appear above:

Variation of formal announcement from both sets of parents:

It is with great happiness that
Eve and Geoffrey Bridges
and
Sonya and Rolfe Hunt
announce
the marriage of their children
Catherine Anne Bridges
and
Derrick Sherwood Hunt
on Saturday, December the eleventh
One thousand nine hundred and ninety-three
Springfield, Kansas

Variation of a formal announcement, from bride and groom only:

Janet Lane Carter and Michael Arthur Shelton
joyfully announce their marriage
on Friday, August the twentieth
One thousand nine hundred and ninety-three
Denver, Colorado

Note-style announcement, written by bride to acquaintances, with name-change indication:

Dear Mr. and Mrs. Keith Hamilton,

It is with great joy that I write to let you know that Douglas Riley and I were married on Saturday, May the fifteenth of this year,[*] in Glen Valley.

We hope to be seeing you sometime soon.

Sincerely,
VALERIE (HESSEL) RILEY[**]

Note-style announcement, written by groom to good friends who know the bride, with indication of bride's current preferred name:

Dear Jane and Jerry,

I am delighted to let you know that Marilyn and I were married on Sunday, November the seventh of this year, in Palomar, Arizona. Marilyn will continue to be known as Marilyn Grace Lockesley.[***]

We're both very happy and look forward to seeing you soon.

Love,
MARK

* The note should bear the date of composition in the upper right-hand corner. If the wedding was the previous year, the note should say "last year."

** If the bride were now using her former last name as her middle name, parentheses would not be necessary. If the bride were keeping her former name, she would simply sign "Valerie Hessel."

*** If Marilyn were adopting her husband's last name, this line would read, for example, "Marilyn will now be known as Marilyn Grace Halliwell."

Note-style announcement, written by bride's mother to intimate friends:

Dear Shirley and Ed,
   Frank and I especially wanted you to know that our daughter Jeanne was married to Chad Solis on Saturday, September the twenty-fifth of this year, in Friendship, Ohio.
   We are very pleased and look forward to introducing them to you soon.

As always,
ELAINE

INFORMAL ACKNOWLEDGMENTS

An informal invitation to a wedding does not have to be acknowledged unless it's specifically requested (e.g., by "Please reply" or "R.s.v.p."), the invitation is also to a reception, or the wedding is taking place in a private home. An informal wedding announcement does not have to be acknowledged unless you wish to do so.

When acknowledging an informal invitation, try to repeat the format of the invitation as closely as possible. If accepting, you need to repeat only the date and time of the occasion. It is not necessary to repeat the place. If extending your regrets, you need to repeat only the date. You don't need to express your reason for not attending, although it's a courteous thing to do when responding informally.

Wedding presents should be sent or delivered *independently* of invitation acknowledgments. When acknowledging a wedding announcement, you may send an accompanying gift if you so desire, but it's not customary. For sample notes to accompany wedding presents—or to acknowledge a wedding announcement—see chapter 6.

Here are examples of different kinds of informal acknowledgments, based on the informal invitations appearing above:

Acceptance to a variation of a formal invitation (handwritten in black ink):

Neil and Milly Harcout
joyfully accept
Janet Lane Carter and Michael Arthur Shelton's
kind invitation for
Friday, August the twentieth
at half after five o'clock

Regrets to the same invitation:

Because they will be out of the country,
Neil and Milly Harcout
are very sorry that they cannot accept
Janet Lane Carter and Michael Arthur Shelton's
kind invitation for
Friday, August the twentieth

Acceptance to a note-style invitation from the groom, a good friend, requesting that replies be sent to the bride's mother:

Dear Mrs. Lockesley,
   My husband, Jerry, and I accept with pleasure Marilyn and Bob's invitation for Sunday, November the seventh, at seven o'clock. We look forward to seeing you there.

Sincerely,
JANE WALLACE

If replies were to have been sent directly to the groom, the acceptance note might have read as follows:

Dear Mark,

Jerry and I are delighted to accept the invitation from Marilyn and you for Sunday, November the seventh, at seven o'clock.

We'll be the ones smiling from ear to ear!

Love,
JANE

Regrets to a note-style invitation from the bride's mother, an intimate friend:

Dear Elaine,

I deeply regret that Ed and I won't be able to accept Jeanne and Chad's kind invitation for Saturday, September the twenty-fifth, due to a previous engagement. Please give them our best wishes.

My love to you and Frank.

Yours,
SHIRLEY

FIVE

Thank-you Notes and Letters

THE ESSENTIAL PURPOSE of a thank-you note or letter is to give the recipient a tangible token of your gratitude for his or her thoughtfulness. It should be written as promptly as possible. Length is not a critical factor, but timeliness is.

If you are especially busy when a thank-you note or letter is warranted, write a brief message rather than procrastinate. In relatively formal acknowledgments, a two- or three-line note is perfectly acceptable. In relatively informal acknowledgments, the type sent to people with whom you are more familiar, a longer note or letter is always appreciated, but one or two paragraphs will suffice, especially when written upon or accompanied by an attractive card.

Assuming you are writing a letter that communicates other information besides thanks, be sure to express your thanks first, then proceed with the rest of the letter. In a formal thank-you letter, thanks should be expressed in the first line. In an informal thank-you letter, it's fine to start more indirectly, but your thanks should be mentioned within the opening paragraph.

WHEN TO SEND A THANK-YOU NOTE OR LETTER

Feel free to respond to even the simplest favor, gift, or courtesy with a thank-you note or letter. Everyone appreciates receiving kind words in the mail. From a social perspective, however, there are some occasions that warrant a thank-you note or letter more than others. The following chart distinguishes between occasions when a thank-you note or letter is socially expected and occasions when it is optional:

Situation	Expected	Optional
Dinner or party	if you were guest of honor	if you thanked host when leaving
Hospitality, overnight or longer	always	
Gift	for wedding gifts	for all but wedding gifts, if you thanked donor upon receipt
Helpful action	if solicited by you in writing or in a public forum	if not solicited by you in writing or in a public forum, and if you thanked benefactor promptly
Condolence or congratulation card or letter	always, except for printed cards without a personal message	
Birthday card or get-well letter		generally, although a very thoughtful card or letter deserves response

THANK-YOU FOR A DINNER, PARTY, OR EVENT

FORMAL

In response to a formal gathering, such as a black-tie reception or a banquet, a formal tone in a brief note is appropriate for thanking someone with whom you were not previously acquainted. This is the correct social procedure even if you managed to become quite friendly with your host in the course of the gathering. If you were well acquainted with your host *before* the gathering, this same formal approach in a thank-you note would remain appropriate, although not mandatory. A thank-you note that properly reflects the tone of the occasion is always in good taste.

In the following example, written in response to a formal dinner given by a college dean at the start of an academic year, notice how the writer retains a properly formal tone by using the surnames of the hosts in the greeting, by specifying the date of the event, and by not presuming to compliment the hosts on particular aspects of the evening:

> Dear Dr. and Mrs. Stone,
> My husband Mark and I wish to thank you for a delightful evening August 3. It was very kind of you to extend your hospitality to us and to give us the pleasure of meeting your friends and colleagues.
> Our best wishes to you for a glorious year.
>
> > Very truly yours,
> > KARLA ANDERS

Here are some other examples of formal thank-you notes for a dinner, party, or event:

To a friend's relatives (married with different last names), after a dinner dance:

> Dear Mr. Panelli and Ms. DeVoe,
> I had a wonderful time last Saturday evening at your party. I'm very grateful to you for welcoming me into your home, and to my good friends Ted and Valerie Thurston for enabling me to meet you.
>
> > Sincerely yours,
> > MYRON BLACK

To an executive at the writer's place of business and her husband, after an anniversary party:

> Dear Mr. and Mrs. Forstner,
> Thank you for including my husband Stefan and me in the celebration of your twenty-fifth anniversary. Being a part of such a festive occasion was an honor and a joy.
>
> > Yours truly,
> > LEE PASCALE

INFORMAL

A relatively informal event hosted by people with whom you are, or hope to become, more familiar, calls for a slightly longer, less formal note. The writer personalizes the following note by referring to particular aspects of the evening that were memorable to him and by offering his readers a glimpse into his private world:

Dear Beth and Don,

Last night's dinner was great! Thanks for inviting me and for introducing me to the wonders of Malaysian cuisine. It was a most welcome and exotic break from a week of quick meals between long hours of work.

Please say hello to Barbara for me, and let her know how much I enjoyed our talk about Ireland. It's even inspired me to look into travel possibilities.

Best wishes,
MIKE

Here are some other examples of informal thank-you notes for a dinner, party, or event:

To previously unfamiliar relatives of a friend, for a surprise birthday party on behalf of that friend:

Dear Hope and Lionel,

You are to be congratulated for pulling off a wondrous surprise and a magnificent party! I've never seen Evelyn enjoy herself more, and the spirit was contagious. She is truly blessed to have such loving, creative, and fun people in her family.

Evelyn is a dear friend, and it meant a lot to me to be able to share an important event in her life. Thank you for your kindness toward me and for the way that you made all of Evelyn's friends feel special.

Cordially,
DANIEL GILBERT

To an employer and his wife for an outdoor barbecue:

Dear Denise and Mario,
    Bob and I are still talking about what a good time we had at last Thursday's barbecue. It was the perfect way to spend a gorgeous summer evening.
    Thanks for having us over. And thanks, also, for sharing with us the recipe for your delicious barbecue sauce! It will bring more flavor to our summer, not to mention pleasant memories.

Yours,
MERRILEE

THANK-YOU FOR HOSPITALITY OVERNIGHT OR LONGER

If you have stayed overnight or longer with someone, it is always appropriate to adopt a relatively informal tone in your thank-you note or letter. To do otherwise might appear cold, given the extent to which you've been allowed to share your host's personal domain.

In the following example, the writer, a good friend of the recipient, is thoughtful enough not only to refer to specific nice moments during her stay, but also to satisfy her host's natural curiosity about her return home:

Dear Sara,
    Spending time with you is always a pleasure, and I'm particularly grateful for last weekend. Thanks for the good food, the good bed, the good companionship, and the good laughs!
    As you suggested, I took the long, leisurely route back home and saw some beautiful fall foliage. Now I'm back in the gray city, remembering our lunch in your sunny garden and my afternoon nap with your cat Max. It all went by too fast!
    Please keep in touch, and give serious thought to visiting me in Boston.

Your friend,
KIM

In the following thank-you note, written to hosts who were not previously known by the writer, the tone is appropriately more reserved, but still informal:

Dear Dale and Jerry,
    Thank you for welcoming Barbara and me into your home this past weekend, and for all you did to make us feel so comfortable. Our visit to Santa Fe was doubly pleasant for having been able to meet you and for having been able to relax in such gracious surroundings. Best of luck with your remodeling plans.

Sincerely,
BILL

Here are some other examples of informal notes thanking hosts for overnight or longer hospitality:

To friends who put their vacation home at the writer's disposal, but who were not present during his stay:

Dear Arlene and Sam,
    Having just returned from a glorious, life-restoring weekend in the Adirondacks, I wanted to write to say how grateful I am to you for letting me stay at your cabin. It was very kind of you and much appreciated.
    No wonder you're so fond of the place! The views are truly spectacular. The whole time I was there, I entertained myself simply watching the light change on the mountains during the course of the day and hiking the trails that ran down to the river. The laurel was in full bloom, and I felt like a king having it all to myself.
    I look forward to thanking you in person when you return from California.

All my best,
GARY

To acquaintances who hosted the writer and her husband—as well as several other couples—after an outing:

Dear Sue and Marshall,
    You couldn't have been nicer or more hospitable to Peter, me, and the rest of the group this past Friday night. Many thanks for making us feel so welcome!

Please give our special thanks to your daughter Shana for lending us her bed. It was an unexpected treat to sleep not only under a canopy of stars, but also in a teenager's room that was so well kept!

You have a charming family and a lovely home. Thanks again for sharing them with us.

Sincerely,
HANNAH

THANK-YOU FOR A WEDDING GIFT

FORMAL

Generally speaking, a formal thank-you note for a wedding gift is written by the bride either before or after the wedding. Assuming the bride will be changing her name with the marriage, she should sign her former name if she writes the thank-you note *before* the wedding and her new, married name, followed by "(Mrs.)," if she writes the note *after* the wedding. If the bride will not be changing her name, then the signature on the note should be the same, regardless of whether the note is written before or after the wedding.

When writing to acknowledge a wedding gift from someone who is not a friend or relative, the writer should use the surname of the giver in the greeting, refer to the specific gift given, and offer a general remark about its usefulness.

In the following example, written *after* the wedding, the writer signs with her new married name, indicated by writing "(Mrs.)" after the signature:

Dear Mr. and Mrs. Roth,

David and I are delighted with the lovely clock you sent us. It will have an honored place in our new home.

Thank you for your thoughtfulness. I hope we will have a chance to express our gratitude in person sometime soon.

Sincerely yours,
MARY SIMMS (Mrs.)

Assuming Mary Simms had written this note *before* the wedding, when she used the name "Mary Schaeffer," she would have signed it simply "Mary Schaeffer."

Here are more examples of formal thank-you notes for wedding presents:

To a mother's business associate with whom the writer is not well acquainted:

Dear Mr. Delaney,
    Thank you very much for giving Larry and me the beautiful cedar sculpture on the occasion of our wedding. We both like natural wood objects, so it was an especially appropriate gift, and a joy to receive.
    My mother joins Larry and me in sending you our best regards.

Yours truly,
Paula Jensen (Mrs.)

To acquaintances who belong to the same social group:

Dear Mr. and Mrs. Hammermoor,
    The exquisite embroidered towels you gave to my fiancé, John Kincaid, and me as a wedding present are very much appreciated. Their early American design will fit perfectly in our new home.
    Please accept our gratitude and best wishes.

Sincerely yours,
Janice Muldane

INFORMAL

When writing a thank-you note for a wedding gift to someone who is a friend or relative, use first-person address and adopt a casual, enthusiastic tone. Always refer specifically to the gift, and allude as specifically as you wish to your plans for using the gift. Here are a couple of examples:

To a good friend:

Dear Jan,
    Thank you so much for the cobalt blue glasses! They'll look beautiful on our dinner table, as I hope you will soon discover for

yourself. Ralph is especially appreciative. How did you know that cobalt blue is one of his favorite colors?

You'll have to solve that mystery later, when Ralph and I get back from Florida. We'll always value your gift, Jan, as well as your friendship.

Love,
KELLY

To relatives:

Dear Aunt Becky and Uncle Gene,

Tom and I love the stoneware bookends you gave us as a wedding gift. We plan to use them to hold our favorite books of poetry: Browning for me, Frost for Tom—a good way to start off our new life together. Every time we look at the bookends, we'll recall how very special you are.

Best wishes from both of us!

Love,
ANNETTE

THANK-YOU FOR A GIFT OF MONEY

When thanking someone for a monetary gift, be sure to mention the exact amount sent and how you intend to spend it. Do not merely say that you are saving the money. Instead, let your recipient know that his or her money is being put to good use—a use that you feel will please the recipient.

FORMAL

In writing to someone whom you do not know very well, it is best to be brief but sincere, avoiding remarks that are overly effusive or too personal. Consider the following example, written to a friend of a friend:

Dear Mrs. Weaver,

Thank you for your $50 check. I'm using it to buy a brand-new set of camel-hair brushes for oil painting. I've been wanting these brushes for some time. It was very kind of you to think of me, and I will think of you whenever I use my new brushes.

Sincerely,
CARLY SHOOP

INFORMAL

An informal note thanking a friend or relative for a monetary gift can be more personable and effusive, like the following example:

Dear Chad and Mandy,
What a treat it was to get your $100 check! Now I can start prowling the sporting-goods stores until I find just the right rack for the back of my bike. It's friends like you who make the nicest things possible!

I'm looking forward to seeing you next month at the Bear Lake picnic. Meanwhile, give the kids some big hugs from me.

Love,
PAUL

THANK-YOU FOR A KIND ACTION

Thank-you notes or letters are not appropriate for *every* act of kindness that someone bestows upon you. Save them for special acts of kindness, such as favors that are extended to you by people whom you do not know well or the thoughtful deeds of friends that go beyond the normal kindnesses characterizing your day-to-day relationships with one another. The former situation calls for a formal, but gracious, acknowledgment. The latter situation calls for a more informal approach.

FORMAL

In this example of a note written to the father of a son's classmate, the writer is careful to explain the circumstances prompting the letter without implying that the recipient might not readily recall them:

Dear Mr. Weidner,
    I am writing to let you know how much I appreciate your helping
my son Robert last Thursday when he sprained his ankle. It meant a
great deal to him to have someone extend comfort and care at such a
distressing time.
    Robert's ankle is healing well, and he should be his normal, active
self again in about a week. He joins the rest of my family in
thanking you for your kindness.

Very truly yours,
PHILIP CANOFF

INFORMAL

An informal note thanking a friend for doing an exceptional favor
is always appreciated, even if you've already thanked the friend in
person. In the following example, the writer is careful not to em-
barrass her friend by overdramatizing matters or by adopting too
serious a tone:

Dear Emily,
    One of the most wonderful parts of my trip was returning home
to find everything looking so shipshape. I just had to thank you
again for watching over things so well while I was away. You did a
great job! I only hope that my plants don't miss you now that I'm
back.

Your grateful neighbor,
LYNN

THANK-YOU FOR A NOTE OR LETTER
OF CONGRATULATIONS

FORMAL

Congratulations from someone with whom you are not well acquainted can be acknowledged formally with a very simple, gracious note, as follows:

Dear Mr. and Mrs. Bresslin,
    I very much appreciate your congratulations on my recent
promotion to vice president. Your kind words made the occasion all

the more meaningful to me. Thank you for taking the time to be so thoughtful.

Very truly yours,
JUSTINE MARKS

INFORMAL

An informal note or letter acknowledging the congratulations of a friend or relative is best kept light and affectionate, as in the following example:

Dear Mary,
Thanks for sending me such a sweet note on my graduation. You're right—I have the whole world at my feet, and it's making me mighty dizzy! It's good to know there are such dear and kind people as you near at hand.

All my best,
TRACY

THANK-YOU FOR A NOTE OR LETTER OF CONDOLENCE

Condolences should always be acknowledged in a timely manner. However, if the actual recipient is indisposed to write thank-you notes, it's perfectly acceptable for any other member of the family to do so. In such a case, the writer should not feel compelled to explain why the actual recipient of condolences isn't writing or to apologize for that person. In fact, it would be inappropriate. Formal and informal examples of both types of thank-you notes are given below.

FORMAL

A thank-you for a condolence note sent by someone with whom you are not very familiar should be formal and brief. If the surname of the deceased differs from the surname of the writer, the writer should discreetly mention the deceased's name in the note, as in the following example:

Dear Mr. and Mrs. Donaldson,
   My family and I are very grateful to you for your kind words of sympathy on the death of my father, Lemuel Shawn. It is comforting to know that you remember him kindly.

                                   Kindest regards,
                                   CATHERINE OSTLEY

The following note is an example of a formal thank-you note written by someone in the family other than the recipient of the condolence note (in this case, a cousin of the recipient). Notice how the writer clearly and concisely communicates the names and relationships of all parties involved:

Dear Mr. and Mrs. Ulanoff,
   On behalf of my cousin, Keith Herde, I am writing to thank you for expressing your sympathy over the loss of his mother and my aunt, Melanie Baker. Your thoughtfulness at this time of sorrow in our family is appreciated by all of us.

                                   Sincerely yours,
                                   MICHELLE LINSTROM

INFORMAL

A note or letter acknowledging the condolences of someone who is close to you should reflect that closeness without being maudlin, as in the following example:

Dear Ty,
   I was very touched by your note to me after my Aunt Margie died. It was a trying time for me, and I often drew support by thinking of you and your many kindnesses. Thanks for sharing with me your memories of Aunt Margie's Sunday brunches. They were fun times for everyone. And thanks for being so compassionate.

                                   Your friend,
                                   KAREN

The following note is an example of an informal thank-you written by someone other than the recipient of the condolence note (in this case, a brother). In this type of informal thank-you note, the familiar form of greeting is appropriate, even if the writer is not personally acquainted with the recipient.

Dear Peggy,

    My sister Linda has asked me to tell you how grateful she is for your kind words of sympathy on the death of our father. Your support means a great deal to her. I'm thankful she has a good friend like you in her corner.

    As soon as matters settle down, Linda will be talking with you herself. In the meantime, we are all bearing up as well as can be expected at such a sad time.

    My best wishes to you and your family.

Sincerely,
FRANK DiCONTI

Here are more examples of informal thank-you notes for condolences, written by the actual recipients of the condolence notes:

To good friends after the death of a spouse:

Dear Suzanne and Richard,

    You were always very precious people to Helen and me. Now that Helen is gone, you are all the more dear to me. Thank you from the bottom of my heart for all your sympathy and support during these past few difficult weeks.

    I know you join me in missing Helen, and I hope you, like me, draw comfort from remembering our happy times together. I look forward to seeing you again very soon.

Love,
STEWART

To an acquaintance after the death of a parent:

Dear Hank,

    Thank you for your thoughtful words of sympathy on the death of my mother. I, too, wish you had met her. She was a woman of many talents and interests, and I'm sure you would have liked each other. Pam and I both miss her now very much.

Our best wishes to your family.

Sincerely,
O<small>SCAR</small>

SIX

Notes and Letters of Congratulations

FEW ITEMS of correspondence are easier to write and more likely to be well received than notes or letters of congratulations. Therefore, it's wise to take advantage of every opportunity to write one: a graduation, a promotion, an award, an engagement, a marriage, a birth, an adoption, or any major accomplishment or milestone in the recipient's life. Written congratulations are obligatory only when the recipient him- or herself has written to you about the cause for congratulations. Nevertheless, they are always appropriate.

A short note is sufficient for virtually any situation that warrants congratulations, whether it's a formal note to a business associate or an informal note to a family member. All that you need to do in the note is to cite the occasion, express your happiness, and extend your best wishes.

Informal congratulations can be letter-length, elaborating on the cause for congratulation or reminiscing about the past leading up to that cause. Just remember that it's best to stay focused on the theme of congratulation throughout the letter, rather than shifting to other topics. A recipient who deserves congratulation also deserves a letter that's devoted to that purpose alone. If you want to write about other matters, do so in another letter.

CONGRATULATIONS ON A GRADUATION

FORMAL

A formal note of congratulations on a graduation is appropriate if you are writing to someone whom you do not know well on a personal basis. It is *not* appropriate if you think that you might have to identify yourself within the note in order for the recipient to recognize your name. If you are acquainted with the graduate's parents but have never met the graduate him- or herself, you should address your note to the parents and request that your congratulations be conveyed to the graduate.

A formal note of congratulations to a graduate should be very brief. You can address the recipient either by first name or last name (whichever is more comfortable to you), but you should sign your full name, as in the following examples:

Dear Miss O'Brien,

My friend Kevin Mills told me about your graduation from Colby College. Please accept my congratulations on your fine achievement. I hope that the years ahead are successful and fulfilling ones.

Yours truly,
ROBERT PASCO

Dear Shelley,

I was happy to hear that your daughter Kathleen is about to graduate from Ohio State University. You must be very proud of her.

Please give Kathleen my congratulations and my best wishes for the future.

Sincerely,
MYRA STERN

INFORMAL

An informal note or letter congratulating a graduate can be brief and to the point, but should reflect genuine warmth and enthusiasm. Notice how the following examples refer directly and amiably to the bond between the sender and the recipient:

To a niece:

Dear Janine,
Congratulations on your graduation! I remember reading and rereading *Winnie the Pooh* to you fifteen years ago, at your insistence. You were an eager learner then, and now you're a full-fledged scholar.
All the best to you in the years to come. Knowing how clever and conscientious you are, I'm sure you'll do well.

Love,
Uncle LEW

To a good friend:

Dear Andy,
Finally, after all your hard work, the day has come. Many congratulations, graduate! I'm very proud of you, and grateful for our friendship over these past years.
I hope you receive all the good fortune you deserve. Please don't hesitate to call if I can help you in any way.

Best wishes,
PAM

If you are sending a gift with your congratulations to a graduate, you should allude to this fact in your note or letter. It prepares your reader to receive the gift more appreciatively, and it prevents misunderstandings in case the gift is accidentally missing.
See how the thoughtfulness of each of the following congratulations is enhanced by a brief, tactful mention of the accompanying gift:

To a good friend:

Dear Rachel,
Your graduation from Elmira gives me so much joy and pride. It's an outstanding achievement! Please accept my heartfelt congratulations, along with the enclosed book: one that made me

think of you and that I hope you'll enjoy. With this gift goes my deep affection and admiration.

May the future bring you everything you desire!

Love,
ROSE

To a nephew:

Dear Jason,

What a pleasure it is to congratulate you on your graduation! You put so much time and effort into reaching your goal, and now you've done it! Please give yourself a pat on the back for me, and a special treat (I'm enclosing some encouragement).

You have a wonderful life ahead of you, Jason, and I know you will make the most of it.

Love,
Uncle MIKE

CONGRATULATIONS ON A PROMOTION, ACHIEVEMENT, OR AWARD

FORMAL

Like any formal note of congratulations, a note regarding a promotion, achievement, or award should be sent only to someone who will have no difficulty recognizing your name. It is best to use full names in the greeting and in the signature.

Also, avoid referring to the promotion, achievement, or award as one that the recipient explicitly "deserves"—a judgment that can appear presumptuous from someone who is not intimately acquainted. Instead, reference to the recipient's merits should be made more generally, as in the following examples:

Dear Mr. Fahrbach,

I was delighted to read in the *Jamestown Journal* about your Citizen's Award. For the past ten years, your contributions to the community have been uniquely generous and effective, and it's good to see them acknowledged with such a high honor.

Please accept my congratulations and best wishes.

Sincerely,
ALLEN EARLE

Dear Ms. Rousse,

Congratulations on your recent promotion to Vice President of Operations at Telemat. Your dynamic style of leadership will be a major asset in that position.

I look forward to a great future for you and for the company.

Best wishes,
BRIAN WILLIAMS

Dear Mr. Schoner,

Allow me to congratulate you on your inspirational speech to the Partners' Club last Thursday night. Your points in favor of supporting election reform were very convincing and well expressed. I'm sure they will have a positive impact on the upcoming vote.

Gratefully yours,
LENA MOORE

INFORMAL

An informal note congratulating someone on a promotion, achievement, or award should be sincere and straightforward. Being someone who knows the recipient fairly well, you can feel free to refer to the honor as something that the recipient genuinely deserves.

This is not the occasion to tease, to be sarcastic, or to take any credit away from the person to whom you're writing. Concentrate on your happiness about the honor and on the recipient's merits contributing to that honor.

Here are a couple of examples of informal notes of congratulation:

Dear Jerry,

What a joy it is to drive down Yancy Boulevard and see your new office there. It looks great. May it bring you all the success you deserve after helping so many people (including me) find homes to match their dreams.

My hearty congratulations to you, Jerry! Give me a call, and we can work out a time to celebrate together.

Sincerely,
FRANK

Dear Elaine,

Congratulations on your promotion! Marty and I are bursting with pride for you and very happy that all your hard work is being rewarded. You're a real credit to Lanner and Company, and a wonderful friend as well!

Love,
CHRIS

CONGRATULATIONS ON AN ENGAGEMENT OR MARRIAGE

FORMAL

A formal note of congratulations on an engagement or marriage should be addressed to the person in the couple with whom you are better acquainted. If you are equally acquainted with both parties, then the note should be sent to the prospective bride or wife (when writing to a wife, it's customary to address her as "Mrs.," followed by the husband's last name, unless you know otherwise).

According to tradition, the specific word "congratulations" is addressed only to the prospective groom or husband, in which case it implies, "Congratulations on receiving a 'yes' answer to your proposal." It is considered impolite to address the prospective bride or wife with the word "congratulations," because the unflattering implication would be, "Congratulations on attracting a proposal." Instead of being literally congratulated, the prospective bride or wife is customarily extended "best wishes."

It is generally considered inappropriate to send a gift along with formal congratulations, except in two situations: (1) you have already received and answered a formal wedding invitation, or (2) you have received a formal wedding announcement and are using this occasion to respond to it. In these two situations, you may choose either to send a gift along with your note of congratulations or simply to send a note, depending on your personal inclination.

Here are examples of formal notes of congratulations:

Dear Mr. Clawson,

Howard Shilte informed me about your engagement to be married to Miss Tucker. Please accept my congratulations. I wish both of you a wonderful life together.

Yours truly,
PETER NESS

———

Dear Miss Belotti,

I was happy to read in the *Lesterville News* that you are engaged to be married to Mr. Crimi. My husband and I have enjoyed the friendship of your Aunt Linda and Uncle Ned for many years, and we're delighted at this latest cause for celebration in their family. My very best regards to you and your fiancé.

Sincerely,
JESSICA KERRY

———

Dear Mrs. Inchnor,

Having recently learned of your marriage, I wanted to write to say how pleased I was. My husband, Richard, joins me in wishing you every possible happiness.

Please give our congratulations to your husband.

Very truly yours,
DIANA McCARR

INFORMAL

Like a formal note of congratulations on an engagement or a marriage, an informal note or letter should be addressed to the person in the couple whom you know better or, if they are equally familiar, the prospective bride or wife. However, you may want to write each person separately, especially if you are very close to one or both of them. If writing to someone whom you do not know (the prospective spouse or spouse of a friend or relative), keep in mind that it is impolite to refer to him or her as "lucky."

Like a formal note, an informal note or letter customarily uses the word "congratulations" when addressing the man, but not when addressing the woman. In the latter situation, the extension of "best wishes" is traditionally more acceptable.

It is not appropriate to send a gift with informal congratulations on an engagement. A gift may be sent with informal congratulations on a marriage; however, it is not common practice. Usually, a gift is given only after one has received and answered a wedding invitation.

If a gift does accompany your informal note or letter of congratulations, you should discreetly allude to that fact (see an example of this kind of letter below).

To a good friend on her engagement:

Dear Myra,

I just wanted to write and let you know how thrilled I am about your engagement to David. You are dear to me and a wonderfully loving person, so it is a blessing to know that you have found someone with whom you want to share your life.

I look forward to meeting David soon and to offering both of you my very best wishes in person.

Love,
JACK

To a niece's fiancé, whom the writer has not met, on their engagement:

Dear David,

As Myra's aunt, I would like to congratulate you on your engagement and welcome you into our family.

Myra has always been a source of pride and pleasure to us, and I am delighted at this latest good news. Rest assured, you come very well recommended. Myra sings your praises to one and all!

My sister tells me that you'll be visiting Newtown next month. I can't wait to see you then and thank you for making my niece so happy.

Best wishes,
ANN JOHNSTON

To a good friend, on his marriage, with a gift:

Dear Kyle,

Thank you for writing to Sally and me about your recent marriage. Rita sounds like a lovely person, and you sound quite happy in your new life. All in all, it was a wonderful letter to read, and we salute the two of you!

Please come visit us anytime that's convenient. We'll break out the champagne and good china! Meanwhile, we're sending you and Rita something to remind you of our love and good wishes.

Love,
STEVE

CONGRATULATIONS ON THE BIRTH OR ADOPTION OF A BABY

FORMAL

A formal note of congratulations on the birth or adoption of a baby should be very brief and general. The parents should be addressed by last name, and the text of the letter should cite the child's full name, excluding the last name.

It is perfectly appropriate to offer congratulations on the adoption of a child who is just joining the family. However, it is not appropriate to offer congratulations on an adoption if the child has been living with the family for a year or more prior to the adoption, unless the family makes a public announcement regarding that adoption (e.g., a formal note to you).

It is not customary to send a gift with a formal note of congratulations. However, if you do send a gift, you should refer to it discreetly within your note (see example below).

Here are examples of formal congratulatory notes on a birth and on an adoption:

To parents on a birth:

Dear Mr. and Mrs. Gunther,

My husband, Tim, and I were delighted to hear about the birth of your son, Anthony Junior. Please accept our congratulations on this happy occasion.

Very truly yours,
SHARON ELLIS

To parents of a newly adopted child, who have different last names, with a gift:

Dear Mr. Harrington and Ms. Louden,
 Congratulations on the arrival of your daughter Frances Marie into your family. Please accept this welcoming gift on her behalf, along with our best wishes for a wonderful future together.

Sincerely yours,
ELLEN BAKER

INFORMAL

An informal note or letter offering congratulations on a birth or adoption can be as warm and effusive as you want it to be. Assuming you already know the child's name, mention it in the text—if only to verify it, indirectly, with the parents. Otherwise, feel free to ask the baby's name. If you are sending a gift with the note or letter, refer to that gift casually in the text.

 Here are examples of informal congratulatory notes on a birth and on an adoption:

To good friends, on an adoption, with a gift:

Dear Peg and Tom,
 How wonderful it was to hear that you have a new son, Julian! Congratulations all around! I'm sure in his own way Julian already senses how wonderful his parents are and how lucky he is to be a part of such a fine family.

 Please take lots of pictures for posterity, and let me know when it would be convenient for me to visit the three of you. Meanwhile, here's something to help keep Julian warm and cozy.

Love,
BRUCE

To good friends, on a birth:

Dear Vicki and Shawn,
 Many congratulations on the birth of your little girl! I'm so thrilled at the news, I can't even imagine how excited you must be

to have her here after so much planning, waiting, and sheer endurance.

I'm also full of questions: What's her name? What's her coloring? Where will she go to college? And so on, and so forth. As soon as you've had a chance to come back down to earth, give me a call and we'll talk.

My very best wishes to all of you dear people!

Love,
LIANNE

SEVEN

Notes and Letters of Sympathy or Condolence

WRITING TO SOMEONE who is suffering an illness, an injury, a loss of property, or a bereavement may appear at first to be a very daunting task. If you're like most writers in this situation, you are naturally reluctant to acknowledge the recipient's misfortune, you feel helpless to alleviate it, you feel embarrassed about being comparatively better off, and you worry about inadvertently upsetting someone who is already emotionally vulnerable. Yet despite all these concerns, you still feel strongly moved to reach out and comfort your suffering relative, friend, or acquaintance.

In fact, writing a thoughtful sympathy or condolence letter is not, in itself, a difficult task. Certainly it should not have to tax your writing skills. The key to composing such a letter is to be sincere, responding directly to your instinctive need to reach out and offer a few words of comfort, without straining to say "just the right thing." This very simple gesture can prove immensely rewarding, drawing you and your recipient closer together and enabling both of you to face the bad news with more equanimity.

Besides speaking sincerely and not worrying about having something original or magical to say, here are some other important "dos and don'ts" when writing a sympathy or condolence letter:

- DO write as promptly as possible, while your feelings are fresh, and while the recipient can most benefit from reading kind words.

- DON'T feel that you have to justify your writing at such a time or that you have to discuss or even state the specific misfortune involved. A genuine expression of concern for someone's "sorrow" or "troubled times" is always appreciated, and it's all that is necessary.
- DO feel free to be brief. It is truly the thought that counts. In many situations, the recipient won't have the time or energy to give due attention to a lengthy letter. On the other hand, if you feel like visiting on paper with a good friend who is bedridden, or recounting especially cherished memories of a recently deceased friend to his or her spouse, then by all means do so.
- DON'T compare the recipient's misfortunate experience to someone else's, even to your own. Everybody's experience is unique and deserves individual attention.
- DO feel free to express your affection and compassion for the recipient.
- DON'T attempt to distract the recipient from a serious situation with levity, humor, dismissive comments, or upbeat platitudes. The very word "sympathy" (literally, "feeling together") implies that you are willing and able to share in the recipient's sorrow, validating his or her feelings without denying, rejecting, or overriding them.
- DO make a *general* offer to help in any way that you can, provided you sincerely would like to do so. The one exception to the policy of offering general help may be in the case of a note or letter expressing sympathy for a loss of property, when it may be tactless to imply that the afflicted recipient now requires your assistance.
- DON'T offer any *specific* advice or service. Your recipient may or may not be able—or willing—to accept your well-intentioned gesture.

SYMPATHY AT A TIME OF ILLNESS OR INJURY

Although a sympathy note or letter is not obligatory when a relative, friend, or associate is sick or suffering from an injury, it is most definitely appreciated. In situations where the recipient is well known to you and you're reasonably certain that the illness or injury is not too debilitating, it may be appropriate and even therapeutic to follow your initial expression of sympathy with a long, conversational letter that your recipient is likely to enjoy reading. In other situations, brevity is the wisest course.

Notice how the following examples of sympathy notes, addressing a variety of different situations, are consistently soothing to read. They are consoling without offering empty reassurances, and they tactfully acknowledge the general seriousness of the victim's (or caretaker's) plight without calling attention to specific negative aspects—or, worse, possible negative outcomes—of the illness or injury involved.

To a friend who is in the hospital:

Dear Mila,

I was sorry to learn from Lee Zollinger of your illness and hospitalization. It must be quite a trying time for an active and energetic person like you. Your friends and neighbors miss you very much and anxiously await your return home.

My husband, Eric, joins me in offering you our very best wishes for a quick recovery. Please don't hesitate to contact us if there's anything we can do to help.

All the best,
JOAN

To an acquaintance who has been bedridden with heart trouble:

Dear Irwin,

I just wanted to drop you a line to say how sorry I was to hear about your long confinement with heart trouble. Your many kindnesses to me and to the members of the Planner's Club are fondly remembered, and all our prayers are with you for happier and healthier times ahead.

Thank goodness you have a loving and resourceful daughter and son-in-law to help you through this difficult time. My wife, Maureen, joins me in sending them our best regards.

Very truly yours,
JOHN REYNOLDS

To a family member who has been injured in an accident:

Dear Darlene,

Norma and I were shocked to hear about the terrible car accident you suffered and very concerned to learn of the damage it did to your leg and pelvis. Please accept our heartfelt sympathy.

You are a brave and strong woman, Darlene, and we're confident that you'll come through this experience just fine. Yesterday your mother phoned to say that you're healing faster than your doctors expected, which is terrific news!

When you're feeling up to it, please call and let us know how you're doing, and if there's any way we can help you.

Much love,
ARTHUR

To a friend who is taking care of a seriously ill parent:

Dear Lynette,

Word has just reached me of your father's lung cancer and of all the time and energy you've been devoting to his care. I am very sorry that your father has been forced to go through so much pain and hardship, but I know it must be an enormous comfort to him to have you there. You are a wonderfully loving daughter, as well as a real treasure of a friend.

All my best wishes to you and your father. And please, Lynette, call me whenever there's anything I can do, or whenever you feel the need to talk with someone who cares very much about you and about the people who are dear to you.

Love,
NAN

To a friend who has been sick at home with the flu:

Dear Mickey,

I'm so sorry to hear that you're sick with the flu. The world of Inchcliff just isn't as much fun when you're not out and about. I hope that the worst is now behind you and that you'll soon be feeling fitter than ever and ready for racquetball!

If I can help you out in any way, please let me know.

Best wishes,
RANDY

To an acquaintance whose daughter has been injured in an accident:

Dear Mrs. Portland,

   I was very sorry to learn of the accident that your daughter Evelyn suffered last month. I hope she is doing well now.

   Please accept the sympathy of my husband, Frank, and me, and please give Evelyn our best wishes for a swift recovery.

Very truly yours,
SAMANTHA DIFFLY

SYMPATHY REGARDING A LOSS OF PROPERTY

A brief note is a considerate way of expressing your sympathy to anyone who has suffered a major and relatively public loss of property due to calamitous weather, a freak accident, robbery, or vandalism. Just be careful not to ask prying questions, not to overdramatize the dark side of the situation, and not to speculate on possible causes, possible outcomes, or "what-might-have-been" scenarios relating to the tragedy.

Even more than other sympathy notes, this type should be concise and to the point. It should also be sent as soon as possible after you learn about the loss, while the recipient is most in need of support. A note sent several weeks after the loss may unintentionally stir up negative feelings that the recipient is trying to overcome.

When expressing your sympathy for a loss of property, it's a good idea not to offer help—even general help—unless you know the recipient very well and can envision specific needs that you are ready and willing to fulfill. Otherwise, your offer of help may be misconstrued as a tactless offer of charity, as an empty gesture, or (much to your surprise) as a concrete offer.

The following model notes address different kinds of loss situations:

To acquaintances whose house has suffered extensive fire damage:

Dear Louise and Nathan,
    My husband, Barry, and I were saddened to hear that your beautiful home suffered extensive fire damage over Labor Day weekend. We both have wonderful memories of your spring garden party there.
    Our sympathy goes out to you, and we hope that your home will soon be restored to its full beauty.

Sincerely yours,
JILL HOLSTEIN

To a very good friend who has suffered a major theft and to whom the writer feels close enough to suggest different kinds of help he could offer:

Dear Ed,
    I was very sorry to read in this morning's *Franklin Dispatch* about the robbery at your office. It must have been awful for you to walk in and discover what had happened. I hope your loss won't cause you too much hardship.
    I've seen you come through many difficult circumstances with flying colors, so I'm keeping the faith that you'll get through this setback and be all the stronger for it. If you need any help, with cleanup, accounting, office services, or anything else, please don't hesitate to call me.

Love,
AMOS

To a relative whose home has suffered major hurricane damage:

Dear Aunt Rae,
    What a shock it was to hear about the damage done to your house by Hurricane Harry, so suddenly and unexpectedly. Thank goodness you yourself weren't physically hurt!
    I know how much you love that house, and I also know how warm and welcoming it is to visit there. For now, I just want to send you my love and sympathy, along with my very best wishes that

everything can be repaired with the greatest speed and the least amount of trouble. Soon, I hope, I can see for myself that both you and your beautiful home are okay.

Love,
GRACE

CONDOLENCE

Condolence notes or letters are customarily sent to any relative or close friend who has suffered the death of a loved one, even if you have already communicated your sympathy by telephone or in person. However, it is also thoughtful to send condolences to friends or acquaintances who are less familiar to you.

Think of a condolence note as a comforting hand on the shoulder, reminding the recipient that he or she is not all alone in his or her sorrow. As such, the best approach to a condolence message is simple, direct, and sincere, like the sample notes that follow:

To a friend who has lost a spouse:

Dear Ruth,
    I am filled with sorrow over Harold's death. He was a remarkable man and a wonderful friend. I shall always remember our happy weekends together on Lake Morgan and the hilarious stories he used to tell. I miss him very much.
    Please know that you are in my thoughts and prayers these days, and that I sympathize greatly with your loss. You have a special place in my heart, Ruth, and I hope you'll call me if there's any way I can help.

Love,
KIT

To acquaintances who have lost a child:

Dear Mr. and Mrs. Tyler,
    My wife, Susan, and I heard the sad news that your son, Mitchell, died. We are deeply sorry.
    Please accept our sympathy.

Sincerely,
VICTOR BRUNO

To a cousin who has lost a sister:

Dear Jane,

I was shocked when Mom told me about Carol's death. You have my deepest sympathy.

The last time I saw Carol was many years ago, when she was a vibrant, enthusiastic college student with a friendly word for everyone. She will always remain that way in my memories.

Robert joins me in sending you love and best wishes on this very sad occasion.

Love,
PAULINE

To a friend whose parent has died:

Dear Roland,

My thoughts and sympathy are with you at this sad time. I know how close you were to your father, and I recall your many loving comments about how helpful and supportive he was to the people in his life. He was a good man, blessed with a fine son.

Please convey my regards and best wishes to your family.

Sincerely,
ADAM

To relatives who have lost a child:

Dear Rena and Val,

All my sympathies are with you on the death of your daughter Antoinette. I only wish there were more that I could do to help heal the sorrow.

Antoinette was a very dear child. Her smile, her spirit, and her goodness will remain alive in the hearts of everyone who knew her.

Please let me help if there's any way that I can.

Love,
STEPHANIE

EIGHT

Letters of Introduction

A GENERATION or two ago, the phrase "letter of introduction" had a clear meaning in regard to social correspondence. If a friend was traveling somewhere and you had another friend who lived in that area, you would write a letter to the distant friend that would pave the way for the two friends to meet socially. The correct basic protocol for the entire process was as follows:

1. You would write a letter to your distant friend, urging him or her to extend hospitality to your traveling friend. This would be at your instigation. It would be very impolite for the traveling friend to ask you to write such a letter.

You would also be very selective in bestowing this favor. A letter of introduction would socially obligate the recipient to take action on your traveling friend's behalf. It was not the sort of obligation you would want to impose on someone you didn't know well or on someone who might not enjoy your traveling friend's company.

2. You would give the letter you wrote to your traveling friend in an unsealed envelope bearing only the name of your distant friend (not the address) and, below it, the phrase "Courtesy of [your name]." You would also give your traveling friend the address of your distant friend, which presumably your traveling friend would transfer to his or her address book.

If this exchange occurred in person, your traveling friend would be expected to seal the letter in your presence without reading it. If, instead, you were mailing the letter to your traveling friend, you would mail it in the same unsealed envelope, inside the envelope addressed to your friend. Upon receipt, your traveling friend would be expected to seal the envelope containing the letter of introduction.

3. You might then write a "notification" letter directly to your distant friend, explaining what you had done and, perhaps, elaborating on the situation a bit more than you did in your letter of introduction.

4. Your traveling friend would mail your sealed letter of introduction (or have it delivered) to the distant friend, along with a very brief "cover letter" offering a greeting, contact information, and an explanation of the enclosed sealed letter.

General custom would be for the traveling friend to mail the letter about a month to two weeks before his or her arrival at the scene. It would be very impolite for the traveling friend to deliver the letter in person.

5. Upon receipt, the distant friend would be socially obligated to contact the traveling friend and extend some sort of hospitality: an invitation to lunch or dinner, an afternoon of sightseeing, or assistance in making some of the arrangements involved with the traveling friend's stay in that area.

Today, this same procedure is still followed in conservative American social circles and in international society. Thus, if you want to write a letter introducing your traveling friend to an American friend who is sensitive about social etiquette or to a friend living in Europe or Japan (for example)—or if, instead of being the writer, you are the traveling friend in a similar situation—it is wise to respect this procedure. Examples of correspondence relating to this procedure (letters of introduction, notification letters, and cover letters) appear below under the heading "Formal Introductions."

In most contemporary situations, however, a letter of introduction is understood to mean a much less formal and socially binding piece of correspondence. Typically, it involves writing a distant friend directly and describing your traveling friend in positive terms for one or more of the following purposes:

- To ask your distant friend's permission to give his or her telephone number or address to your traveling friend.
- To ask your distant friend to consider contacting your traveling friend at the place where your traveling friend will be staying.
- To ask your distant friend if he or she would be willing to perform some specific service for your traveling friend.

No matter what purpose your informal letter of introduction is meant to serve, it's probably best not to mention to your traveling friend that you're writing your distant friend until after you've received an answer to your letter. Certainly it would not be polite to give your traveling friend the telephone number or address of your distant friend without the latter's permission.

Models of this more prevalent type of correspondence are offered below under the heading "Informal Introductions." There is no standard protocol associated with this kind of a letter of introduction, nor are there informal equivalents of the above-mentioned "notification letter" or "cover letter."

FORMAL INTRODUCTIONS

This section provides models of formal or "traditional" letters of introduction, notification letters, and cover letters. As illustrated by the different examples of letters of introduction below, the actual *tone* of individual letters can vary in formality, depending on how familiar the writer is with the recipient and on the personality of the writer or recipient.

LETTERS OF INTRODUCTION

In the following formal letter of introduction, written to a nonintimate friend, the writer is careful to mention that the traveling friend will be visiting the area for the first time, thereby indirectly suggesting to the distant friend that they might like to do some sightseeing together.

Dear Mrs. Evers,

I am giving Augusta Stipp, a valued friend of mine, this letter of introduction to you. Miss Stipp will be in San Francisco from July 7 until July 23, attending the Meistersinger Festival and seeing the lovely sights of San Francisco for the first time. I'm confident that you'll find her as charming as I do and that she will greatly enjoy making your acquaintance.

My sincere regards and affection to you and your family.

> Very truly yours,
> MARY WESTLOW

In the letter of introduction below, the writer does all that is required without adding any detail, thus leaving the distant friend and the traveling friend free to find out about each other in their own way.

Dear Gus,

A dear friend of mine, Perry Santos, will be arriving in Houston the week of August 3 and staying for about ten days. I am giving him this letter of introduction to you because I'm so sure the two of you will enjoy meeting each other. I hope it finds you at home.

> Best wishes,
> EDWARD

The following letter, while formal in type, is fairly informal in tone, which is appropriate for correspondence between two good friends. Note the use of "My dear" in the greeting. This is the correct intimate form of address in Europe, and it should be used whenever you are writing a good friend who lives there.

My dear Charlotte,

This letter introduces you to very close friends of mine, Mr. and Mrs. Miles Richter (Irene), who will be visiting London during the month of September. Like you, they are enthusiastic art collectors, avid gardeners, and a great deal of fun. I only wish I could be there myself!

> Love,
> JO

Notification Letters

A notification letter is, generally, a more detailed version of a formal letter of introduction, written by the same person to his or her distant friend in order to prepare that distant friend for the eventual receipt of the letter of introduction.

Although you are not obliged to send a notification letter, it is a courteous gesture. It can also influence your distant friend to act even more kindly toward your traveling friend.

Here are examples of notification letters that might be written immediately after the formal letters of introduction that appear above (same order):

Dear Mrs. Evers,

On many occasions in the past we have talked about my young friend Augusta Stipp, a pianist, with whom I often attend concerts. She will be visiting San Francisco this coming July, mainly to attend the Meistersinger Festival, and so I gave her a letter of introduction to you. She will be arriving July 7 and staying until July 23.

Augusta has heard many stories about our happy times together in San Francisco and already feels as if she knows you. I'm sure the two of you will like each other. She is a very warm person with simple tastes, who likes seeing new things and meeting new people. Anything you might be disposed to do to make her visit a pleasant one would be greatly appreciated.

Many thanks! I look forward to seeing you when you visit Boston this fall.

Sincerely yours,
Mary Westlow

Dear Gus,

I've given my friend Perry Santos a letter of introduction to you. He'll be staying in Houston the week of August 3 and perhaps a bit longer.

Perry and I have known each other since college days at Duke, when we were both on the swimming team. Since then, we've become practically like brothers. You'll probably notice many similarities! He's traveled all over the world for his import-export business and has some fascinating stories. I'm sure you'll have no trouble coaxing these stories out of him over dinner at Martino's or drinks at Fountain House, two of the many fine places in Houston I think he'd enjoy.

Thanks,
EDWARD

My dear Charlotte,

Two delightful friends of mine, Miles and Irene Richter, will be staying in London this September, and I have given them a letter of introduction to you. I have long wanted you and the Richters to meet each other and couldn't resist this opportunity to try to arrange matters. They are just as gracious and amusing as you are, so I feel encouraged in my effort, and I would be very grateful for your help in making their trip more memorable.

The Richters and I share a love of gardening, sightseeing, and shopping for antiques. While in London, the Richters especially look forward to touring the art galleries. Their tastes are quite eclectic, so they would most likely be interested in any show or gallery you wanted to recommend. They're also fond of comfortable, old-fashioned dining spots that serve traditional British food, of which you know so many!

Please have a wonderful autumn yourself, and let me know how your harvest fares.

Love,
Jo

COVER LETTERS

When you are forwarding a formal letter of introduction that a friend has given to you, it should be accompanied by a very brief formal cover letter, similar to this example:

Dear Mr. Hedley,

Jerome Miles kindly gave me this letter of introduction to you. I will be staying in New York City until July 17, and I look forward to the opportunity of meeting you. My telephone number at the Viceroy Plaza Hotel is 877-3699, extension 602.

Best regards,
NICK SHERMAN

INFORMAL INTRODUCTIONS

Far more common than the formal letter of introduction is the informal version, which is sent directly to the distant friend, confers no obligation upon that friend, and does not even need to involve the traveling friend, unless by mutual choice.

Here are examples of this kind of correspondence applied to different types of situations:

To a nonintimate friend, asking permission to give her telephone number to a traveling friend:

Dear Miss Schmidt,

A very good friend of mine will be visiting Denver the second and third weeks in June. Her name is Lila Best. She is president of the hospital volunteer group to which I belong and to which you so generously contributed this past Christmas. More to the point, she is a true joy to be around.

Would it be all right with you if I gave Lila your telephone number, so that she might get in touch with you while she's in Denver? Her schedule of visits to different medical organizations may not leave her much free time, and I know that June can be a busy month for you, but it would be nice if the two of you could meet. She enjoys playing golf, so maybe the two of you could play together sometime.

I hope you are doing well. Please give my regards to your husband.

Sincerely,
JUDITH SULLIVAN

To an intimate friend, informing him of the fact that a traveling friend will be visiting his area:

Dear Simon,

I'm writing to let you know that a good friend of mine, Bob Abernathy, will be vacationing near you from March 2 through 14. I think the two of you would really hit it off. Bob loves hiking, fishing, and visiting historical sites, and you're a local expert on all these subjects, as I well know!

If you're inclined to get together with Bob, you can call him where he's staying, at the Mohonk Mountain House just outside New Paltz. I told him I'd be writing you about his visit, but please don't feel obligated to call if it's inconvenient. He's very capable of taking care of himself.

> Best wishes,
> CAL

To a friend, informing her that traveling friends will be visiting her area:

Dear Moira,

Guess what? My best friends here, Jenny and Tom Lippley, will be visiting the Parker County area during the week of October 11. I'd love it if the four of you could get together. You have so much in common, apart from Howard and me. Jenny's a lawyer, Tom's an assistant professor of history at Oklahoma State, they have two sons in high school, and, like you, they're very easygoing.

The Lippleys will be staying at the Ardsley Inn in Dorchester. The phone number there is (777) 905-2253. Don't be concerned if you miss them, or if it's not a good time for you to call. They aren't expecting you to contact them, but I'm sure it would be a most pleasant surprise. They've often heard me talk about you—in glowing terms, of course!

I'll be coming to visit before too long, I hope. Until then, my very best to you and Dale.

> Love,
> ANGIE

To a friend, requesting him to do something specific for a traveling friend:

Dear Misha,

A great friend of mine, Jan Steltzner, will be visiting Minneapolis during the month of December. She would very much like to attend yoga classes, either privately or in a group, while she is there, but won't know her schedule until she arrives. Would you be able to help her make arrangements for classes after she gets there? I know that you've taken yoga classes in the area, and I thought you might have some information or contacts that she could use.

If you can help out in any way, she and I would both appreciate it very much. After December 3, you can contact her at the Glendonton Arms, 544-2221, or with your permission, I can give her your number to call. If you're unable to help, that's quite all right! Thanks, Misha.

Best wishes,
DENNY

NINE

Notes of Personal Apology or Complaint

ONE OF THE MOST DIFFICULT pieces of correspondence to write is the note of personal apology or complaint. Either kind of note requires performing a task we wish we didn't have to perform and doing it with tact and grace when we're feeling acutely awkward. Yet there are many situations when an apology or complaint is advisable, and when writing that apology or complaint is preferable to telephoning or making it in person. Among such situations are the following:

- You attend a social gathering hosted by a friend and participate in a heated argument that disturbs that gathering and is witnessed (or even partially waged) by your host. In this case, a note of apology to your host can clear the air and relieves both of you from having to conduct a clumsy face-to-face reconciliation scene. You might also consider writing similar notes of apology to others involved in the argument, assuming you sincerely feel that you should apologize.
- You need to break a social engagement. If the engagement is very soon, it may be best to telephone the host as soon as you realize you won't be able to fulfill the engagement. If there's sufficient time before the engagement (if, for example, the engagement is to attend a wedding that's several weeks away), a

telephone call may not be necessary. Whether or not you telephone first, a brief note of apology is warranted.

• You fail to meet a social obligation, either knowingly or inadvertently. In this type of situation, it may be best to telephone the host as quickly as possible in order to allay his or her possible concern about your welfare. Whether or not you telephone first, a brief note of apology is warranted.

• An acquaintance or a stranger (for example, a neighbor) does something, or allows something to happen, that upsets you so much that you don't trust yourself to remain calm, collected, and competent in a face-to-face confrontation. In this case, a well-written letter of complaint allows you to be more considerate and objective, and your acquaintance or neighbor to be less embarrassed and defensive.

   The same strategy does not apply, however, if your complaint is aimed at a friend rather than an acquaintance or a stranger. With a friend, it is almost always better—and certainly less impersonal—to talk about the complaint face to face instead of writing a note about it.

• You receive a note of complaint that you feel is justified, in which case you should respond as quickly as possible with a note of apology and, if appropriate, a brief statement about what you plan to do to rectify the situation. The fact that the complainer wrote to you instead of calling you or coming to see you in person suggests that he or she would prefer to handle the matter through correspondence.

When writing any note of apology or complaint, the two main rules are: be quick and be brief. Putting off writing the note or writing at length when you finally take pen to paper is just too risky. The less time you spend nurturing or expressing sensitive feelings, the less likely you are to write something that will later make you feel unduly humiliated (in an apology) or that will offend or alienate your recipient (in a complaint).

Consider, for example, the following apology, written to the host of a formal party by an acquaintance who was overly boisterous at that party. Notice how it manages to be effective and, at the same time, appropriately restrained, taking care not to be disconcertingly precise about the offense or to offer excuses.

Dear Mrs. Howe,
    I know I behaved badly at your party last night, and I am very sorry. It was a lovely gathering, and I sincerely wish I had not allowed myself to act the way that I did.
    Please accept my apology.

Very truly yours,
FRANKLIN GLASS

Aside from being quick and brief when writing a letter of complaint, you should also avoid using angry language that is likely to upset your recipient. Even though it may feel good to you at the time to vent your hostile feelings on paper, you don't want to lose sight of your main objective: to influence your recipient to do something in your favor. Record your anger on a sheet of paper that you can tear up immediately afterward, just before you write your actual note of complaint.

In this note of complaint, written to a neighbor who is not well known to the writer about a pesky dog, notice how the writer politely assumes that the recipient is not yet aware of the cause for complaint and is certain to respond well. This approach greatly simplifies what needs to be said in the body of the letter.

Dear Mr. Everett,
    I hate to disturb you with this letter, but I'm sure you would want to know that your dog Rusty has been wandering onto my property and creating some problems. Flowers have been dug up, my son Michael has been scared, and on a couple of occasions, the trash can has been overturned. I would greatly appreciate your doing whatever you can to keep Rusty from getting into our yard.
    Thanks for your cooperation.

Sincerely,
WALTER JACKSON

Here are examples of other letters of complaint or apology, applying to different situations:

Apology to a good friend for a heated argument at the friend's house:

Dear Deanna,
    I deeply regret any misunderstanding that may have been caused by the way I acted at dinner last night. I simply got carried away and had no right to disturb such a pleasant evening.
    I hope that you can forgive me. Your friendship means a great deal to me.

Sincerely,
CARMEN

Apology to a neighbor who has complained about your dog (see complaint letter above):

Dear Mr. Jackson,
    Thank you for calling my dog Rusty's wandering ways to my attention. I am very sorry about the damage and annoyance you've suffered. Apparently, Rusty is able to leap over the fence around his dog yard, so I am now building it several feet higher. Until it's completed, I will make sure that he is kept on a chain when outdoors.
    I hope this ensures that you won't be bothered by Rusty again. If you are, please don't hesitate to tell me.

Sincerely,
FLOYD EVERETT

Apology to a friend for canceling plans to attend the friend's dinner party, written after a phone call (unlike an apology for bad behavior, this type of apology does *require a brief explanation):*

Dear Ariel,
    Please forgive me for having to bow out of your dinner party last Thursday. My schedule at work is so hectic at this time of year that I couldn't anticipate my having to be away from town on precisely that night.

I'm sorry to have disappointed you and to have missed an evening with friends that I was really looking forward to enjoying.

Affectionately,
KAREN

Apology to a friend's mother, for having to cancel an acceptance to a formal wedding and reception invitation issued in her name (when corresponding as a guest invited to a wedding or reception, it's customary to cite the date, not the nature of the occasion):

Dear Mrs. Betts,

I am very sorry to have to tell you that Sheridan and I won't be able to join you on December the sixth, as we had already indicated. Sheridan's mother is seriously ill, and we'll be helping to take care of her in Knoxville.

Please accept our apologies, and extend our best wishes to Athena and Vincent.

Yours truly,
PATRICIA FRANCIS

Apology to friends for failing to show up at a dinner party:

Dear Gloria and John,

Fred and I are so upset at having missed your dinner party last Monday. Please accept our deepest apologies. While eagerly awaiting it, we completely lost track of the date. It was a stupid thing to do, but all too human!

I hope you'll forgive us, and learn to trust us again.

Sincerely,
BRENDA

Complaint to an acquaintance, about the acquaintance's eight-year-old son teasing the writer's six-year-old son:

Dear Debra,

I've always enjoyed talking with you at PTA meetings and at church, and I have a high regard for your activities in both areas, so I'm taking the liberty of writing you about an issue that is causing me concern.

My son Mike has recently started wearing glasses, and he is very self-conscious about them. Unfortunately, your son Cliff has been heard teasing Mike about the glasses on several occasions.

I can understand a child's temptation to tease, and I'm quite sure Cliff doesn't mean to hurt Mike. But the fact is that teasing about this particular subject does hurt Mike's feelings and makes it harder for him to adjust to wearing his glasses. It would mean a lot to me if you could talk with Cliff and explain this delicate situation to him.

Thanks, and my best wishes to you and your family.

Sincerely,

JAN CLAYMORE

PART THREE

Types of Business and Official Correspondence

TEN

Inquiries, Orders, and Reservations: Requests and Responses

INQUIRIES, orders, and reservations—and responses to them—are among the most straightforward kinds of business letters. In each case, the writer's goal is to be as clear and concise as possible, leaving nothing open to misunderstanding.

Here are more specific guidelines:

- If you're writing an inquiry, order, or reservation and you don't have a specific name for your recipient, use any title that sounds appropriate—e.g., Customer Service Representative, Reservations Manager, Public Relations Director.
- When referring to a product, always give the official name and model number—e.g., "I would like to order one Roadrunner Motorcycle Helmet, model #Y-18-M."
- When referring to multiples of a particular product, first spell out the amount, then enclose the numeral in parentheses—e.g., "Thank you for ordering two (2) Roadrunner Motorcycle Helmets, model #Y-18-M."
- When expressing prices for multiples of the same item, indicate the unit price of the item as well as the total price of the number of units involved. In addition, it helps to underline a total price

figure, not only to distinguish it from any subtotal prices (which are *not* underlined), but also to make it stand out. For example, "I would like to order two (2) Roadrunner Motorcycle Helmets, model #Y-18-M, price: $87.00 each/$174.00 for two."

- When requesting a reply, indicate the address to which the reply should be sent. In standard block, semiblock, and indented business letter formats (see Appendix), the writer's address appears at the top of the letter, and so the writer can say in the body of the letter, "Please reply to me at the above address." It is also permissible to incorporate the return address into the body of the letter, introduced by a phrase like "Please reply to me at this address," or to state the return address immediately below the signature, in which case the writer can say in the body of the letter, "Please reply to me at the address given below."

- Don't forget to give your recipient specific time references, indicating not only the dates of events that you mention and of previous correspondence that you cite, but also the date by which you expect a response (or some similar directive, such as "Please reply as soon as possible.").

- When responding to an inquiry, order, or reservation, try to assume a very positive, thankful tone, as if the inquiry, order, or reservation were a compliment and an indication of ongoing interest—e.g., "Thank you for choosing Hotel Piedmont," and "We look forward to serving you in the future."

This chapter is organized into two sections: "Requests" and "Responses." For other letters that are somewhat similar to the models offered here, see chapter 13, "Sales, Promotional, and Fund-raising Letters."

REQUESTS

LETTERS OF INQUIRY

Here are various types of letters of inquiry, including requests for information, assistance, and specific services:

To a carpeting supplier, from an office manager asking for a price quote (NOTE: *In this type of situation, where personal attention can play a significant role, it is best to address the letter to a specific individual and to frame the request on an "I-you" basis. If you do not know to whom to write, try telephoning the organization and asking for a name.):*

Dear Mr. Pollack,

As the office manager of the Piedmont Guidance Clinic, I am interested in carpeting 3,000 square feet of office space with sisal carpeting. Please send me price quotes (including installation) on the sisal carpeting that you supply. I'd very much appreciate a quick response.

Thank you.

Sincerely,
Evelyn McGraw

To a television station, WTIN, from a viewer seeking more information:

Dear Station Manager:

I am writing in regard to the *Mooney Home Repair Hour* program that WTIN broadcast on Saturday, September 24, 1994, from 3 p.m. to 4 p.m. In that program Merle Mooney refinished a home entertainment armoire with what he called a "high-quality nonshiny stain." Would it be possible for you or for him to send me more information about this stain?

I'd like to know which specific brand was used on that program or which specific brand(s) I could buy that would serve the same purposes. However, if this information is not available, I would appreciate knowing more specifically what to look for and ask for, in order to find the same type of stain in a hardware or paint store.

I'm hoping to use this kind of stain on some bookcases that I will be completing within a month, so a quick reply would be welcome.

Thank you.

Yours truly,
Barbara Geiss

To a friend in a noncompeting business, Anderson Appliance Co., from an automobile dealer seeking marketing help:

Dear Scott,

Assuming it isn't a company secret, would you be willing to tell me the name of the designer who did the Anderson Appliance ads that have been appearing recently in the *Cleveland Herald?* I think they are great, and I would like to see what the same designer could do for Otterbein Autos' print advertising.

Please let me know, if possible, as soon as you can.

Thanks, Scott.

Sincerely,

FRANK

To a state park, from a potential tourist (NOTE: *The writer's address is given in the upper right-hand corner of the letter, above the greeting.*):

Dear Manager:

I am considering visiting Woodland State Park this summer with my family: two adults, an eight-year-old girl, a six-year-old boy, and a five-year-old girl. I would greatly appreciate any information you can send me at the above-mentioned address that describes the park, its facilities, and its summer schedule.

I am particularly interested in knowing more about your accommodations. I would like to camp with my family. However, they are not used to camping, so I would consider staying at a lodge or motel if the camping situation is too rugged. My main questions are:

- How big and how private are the campsites? What is the setting like?
- Are the campsites well equipped with showers and toilets?
- Are you allowed to have campfires, and is wood available?
- Can you reserve campsites in advance? If not, what's the best time during the summer (and during the week and day) to come to the park in order to ensure a good campsite?

I would appreciate a response by March 1, so that I have sufficient time to make my summer travel plans.

Thanks for your attention.

Yours truly,

ANNE CULLIGAN

To a storyteller, from an environmental center planning a celebration and contacting a number of possible storytellers (NOTE: *When soliciting information regarding someone's services, it is not always appropriate to state specifically how you think those services should be performed; for example, you may want to avoid influencing the recipient's response so that you can see what your recipient has to say on his or her own. In some situations, however, including the one reflected below, it may be better to give the recipient a more specific idea regarding what you want so that you reduce the odds of getting an inappropriate response.):*

Dear Ms. Leavit,

Crestview Environmental Center is sponsoring a Summer Solstice Celebration June 18 through 25, and we are very interested in having a storyteller perform sometime during this time period. Mr. Geoff Woodbine, a Crestview volunteer, recommended you. If you would like to be considered, please submit your fee schedule and a brief description of the types of stories you tell and programs you conduct.

At the moment, we envision an evening program of solstice- or nature-oriented stories that appeals to adults as well as children and that lasts for one and a half to two hours. However, we are open to other possibilities as well.

We would appreciate a response by April 10.

Thank you.

Sincerely,
ED RIBBICORT

To a highly desired speaker, from a professional group:

Dear Dr. Gennaro,

The Professional Trainers of North America, a nationwide organization of management trainers, would be very pleased and honored if you would speak at our annual convention this June in Detroit, Michigan. Specifically, we would like you to deliver the keynote address on opening night, Friday, June 10, 1994, at 8 p.m. Our theme for this year is "Motivating Good Performance."

If this is agreeable to you, please let me know your fees, terms, and equipment needs at your earliest convenience.

I sincerely hope to have the pleasure of welcoming you to this year's PTNA convention. Your participation will make it a very exciting and memorable event for all of us.

Very truly yours,
WALTER WEAVER
President

ORDERS

From a consumer who does not have the standard catalog order form, to Zenith Department Store:

Dear Customer Service Representative:
Please send the following Zenith merchandise to me at the address given below:

- two (2) director's chairs, model #3652, with navy blue backs and seats, price: $35.00 each/$70.00 for two
- one (1) "Yard Arm" plant holder, model #C-22, price: $27.00
- four (4) wooden planters, in redwood, model #R-170, price $20.00 each/$80.00 for four

Enclosed is my check for $198.00 ($177.00 plus $21 tax and shipping charges). I expect all of this merchandise to arrive within two weeks. Otherwise, please let me know as soon as possible.

Sincerely,
(signature)
SARA DESMOND
1212 Oasis Road
Phoenix, Arizona 85013
(602) 654-7890

To an efficiency expert, from a business manager responding to the expert's estimate (NOTE: in this particular letter, a contract is enclosed for the recipient's signature. Generally speaking, it is better for the initiator of the contract to withhold his or her signature until after the recipient has signed. For a response to an estimate that does not require a separate contract, see the letter immediately following this one.):

Dear Mr. Morton,
Thank you for your January 18 estimate of $3,200.00 for conducting an efficiency survey of Clayton Glass's production department. I am pleased to inform you that we have decided to retain your services.
Enclosed are two copies of a contract reflecting the terms of this project as outlined in my initial, January 8 request and as reflected in

your estimate. Please sign both copies and return them to me as soon as possible. I will then sign both copies and return one copy to you, along with your advance payment.

We look forward to beginning this project promptly on March 1, as indicated in the contract. If you have any further questions, please don't hesitate to call me.

Sincerely,
KRISTIN SHAW
Business Manager

To a tree surgeon, from a property owner responding to the tree trimmer's estimate:

Dear Mr. Delacourt,

Thank you for responding quickly to my March 24 request for your price to remove six trees and trim four trees on my property at 416 Mill Road in Jefferson. I accept your March 28 estimate of $690.00 for this job and would like you to proceed with the work as outlined in the estimate statement.

Specifically, that work calls for:

- removing three oak trees and three maple trees in the southwest corner of the property (designated by bands of red paint around the trunks);
- trimming four maple trees along the west (front) side of the property, so that they are more attractively shaped, allow more light into the front yard, and do not interlace with each other;
- cleaning up all areas where trees have been removed or trimmed, including (as necessary) filling holes and leveling the ground surface;
- cutting as much wood as possible from the six felled trees and the four trimmed trees into firewood no more than 8 inches thick and 20 inches long;
- completing the job by May 1, 1994 (although the earlier, the better).

I would like work to begin as soon as possible. Please contact me at your earliest convenience so that we can set up a work schedule.

Sincerely,
MARY ELLIS

Reservation Requests

To a resort hotel, from a tourist:

Dear Reservations Manager:
  I would like to reserve a double room, with one large bed for two people, for four nights: Sunday, July 3, through Wednesday, July 6, 1994. Enclosed is my check for $85.00, representing one night's deposit.
  I would prefer a room that is as quiet as possible and has a good view. I plan to arrive around 10 p.m. on the night of July 3, although it could be even later, so I would like my room and a parking space kept available for late arrival.
  Please write to the following address, confirming my reservation as requested:

> Michael Tolitho
> 15 Grenoble Terrace
> San Cremona, CA 96083
> (707) 567-1098

I look forward to hearing from you.

> Sincerely,
> MICHAEL TOLITHO

To a theater manager, from a company desiring a block of tickets:

Dear Reservations Manager:
  I would like to purchase a block of 25 orchestra-section tickets for the Carson Valley Symphony's upcoming series of concerts, "Schubert and His Peers." My preferred dates are as follows:

- first choice: Friday, May 14
- second choice: Friday, May 21
- third choice: Saturday, May 15

Enclosed is my check for $500.00 ($20 orchestra seat × 25 people) and a stamped, self-addressed envelope. Please confirm my reservation as soon as possible.

> Yours truly,
> SAM BOWLES
> Public Relations Director

RESPONSES

Here are responses to letters of inquiry, to orders, and to reservations.

Responses to Letters of Inquiry

To a hotel manager who has asked for a price quote, from a supplier of wallcoverings (NOTE: *In a letter like the one appearing below, in which the writer is offering several different choices for the recipient, it is best if the writer begins with the choice that he or she would most like the recipient to make.*):

Dear Mr. Turrell,

Thank you for your letter of September 3, 1994, requesting a price for 1,600 square feet of Lane-Shields fine wallcovering, plus installation. We can give you the following prices for different wallcovering styles:

- Imperial: $8,200
- Royal: $7,700
- Republic: $6,900

To assist you in making your selection, I am enclosing samples of each of these styles, as well as brochures describing them. Please contact me when you are ready to place your order, and I will make sure that it is filled as efficiently as possible.

Sincerely,
ANTHONY OWEN
Account Representative

To a customer who has requested information that cannot be divulged, from a producer of condiments (NOTE: *Although a person writing this type of letter does not have to explain a "no" answer, this writer effectively does so in a manner that appeals to the recipient's self-interest. The writer also manages to turn the letter into a tactful, low-key promotion piece.*):

Dear Ms. Hardiwick,

Thank you for writing us on August 2 to express your interest in the recipe for Heaven Hollow Cranberry Mustard. We are very proud of this product and pleased that you enjoy it. Unfortunately, we cannot publicly reveal the precise mixture of ingredients that gives our mustard its unique taste.

Please understand our need to protect our recipes so that we can continue to stay in business and to provide our customers with the very best products of their type available in the marketplace.

Because you were so kind to let us know how much you like Heaven Hollow Cranberry Mustard, I am enclosing a catalog that not only describes our full line of delicious mustards, ketchups, salad dressings, spreads, and dips, but also offers a number of easy and delightful recipes for salads, sandwiches, side dishes, and party food.

Thanks again for writing.

> Sincerely,
> DALE LOGAN
> Customer Service Manager

To someone who has asked for a catalog that is not yet available, from a seed and bulb company:

Dear Mr. Harner,

Thank you for your letter of November 18 requesting the Gro-Fast catalog "Flowers with Good Scents." Unfortunately, this catalog is currently being revised, and the new edition won't be printed until January of next year. We will send you that catalog as soon as it's available.

In the meantime, I'm enclosing two other popular Gro-Fast catalogs that offer seeds for beautiful spring flowers at discount prices: "Flower Power" and "Ready, Set, Bloom."

I appreciate your interest in Gro-Fast.

> Sincerely,
> MARTIN D'ALLESANDRO
> General Manager

To a citizen's group, from someone who has been asked to speak (NOTE: *The letter below expresses a "yes" response; the letter after that is a different version of the same letter expressing a "no" response.*):

Dear Ms. DeWitt,

I would be delighted to accept the Overton Historical Preservation Society's kind invitation to speak at their meeting on Thursday, November 17, at 8 p.m. As I understand it, you would like me to speak for approximately one hour, with time for questions and answers, on the subject of preservation legislation. My fee for the engagement would be $500, payable in advance.

Thank you for honoring me with your request. Because of tight scheduling demands, I would appreciate hearing your final decision about engaging my services as soon as possible.

Please don't hesitate to call me if you have any further requests.

Sincerely,
OTTO GRUNER

To a citizen's group, from someone who must decline an invitation to speak (NOTE: *A "yes" version of this letter appears above.*):

Dear Ms. DeWitt,

I am very pleased and honored by the Overton Historical Preservation Society's kind invitation to speak at their meeting on Thursday, November 17. Regrettably, I am already busy on this date and must decline the invitation.

Please don't hesitate to contact me again if another occasion arises when you would like me to speak. Meanwhile, my best wishes go to you and to your fine organization.

Sincerely,
OTTO GRUNER

To a friendly business associate, from a manager who is late in respond-ing (NOTE: *When apologizing to an associate or a client or customer for failure to perform according to reasonable expectations, it is best to offer some kind of explanation, even if it's a very general one. If at all possible, the explanation should not reflect negatively on you or anyone else.*):

Dear Ralph,

Please forgive my delay in responding to your letter of October 10, requesting projected budget figures for the Dynamo project. I was away from my office when your letter arrived, and I have since been waiting for the information you requested to become available. Our budget director, Jim Evans, has just notified me that the projected budget for the Dynamo project will be completed by January 15, at which time I will immediately forward a copy to you.

I regret any inconvenience or concern that the delay has caused you. Please feel free to call me if you have any other questions about the Dynamo project.

Yours truly,
ELLEN

RESPONSES TO ORDERS

To a business client who has submitted an order, from an electronic equipment supplier confirming that order (NOTE: In this type of letter, individual items should be listed as closely as possible to the way in which they were listed by the client in his or her order. Appearing below is a confirmation letter that does not *serve as a formal bill. Appearing immediately after that is a version of the same letter that* does *serve as a formal bill.):*

Dear Ms. Carillo,

Thank you for your February 4, 1994, order (#23341 in our records). I am writing to confirm delivery to you within two weeks from today of the following materials:

- three (3) 50-foot Willensdorf cables (model 45-K), at $205.00 each, for a total of $615.00;
- two (2) Rilko switch boxes (model D), at $156.00 each, for a total of $312.00.

Your bill will arrive with your order and will include a shipping charge of $47.00.

We appreciate your choosing Shaw-King Electronics and look forward to serving your future electronic needs.

Sincerely,
TED RENAULT
Customer Service Manager

To a business client who has submitted an order, from an electronic supplier confirming that order (NOTE: This confirmation letter also serves as a bill. Appearing above is a different version of the same letter that does not serve as a bill.):

Dear Ms. Carillo,

Thank you for your February 4, 1994, order (#23341 in our records). Within two weeks from today, the following materials will be delivered to you as ordered:

* three (3) 50-foot Willensdorf cables (model 45-K), at $205.00 each, for a total of <u>$615.00</u>;
* two (2) Rilko switch boxes (model D), at $156.00 each, for a total of <u>$312.00</u>.

There is a shipping charge of <u>$47.00.</u>

Please consider this letter as your bill for that order, which amounts to a total of <u>$974.00</u>, due by April 1, 1994. Checks or money orders should be made out to "Shaw-King Electronics" and should bear the order number.

We appreciate your choosing Shaw-King Electronics and look forward to serving your future electronic needs.

Sincerely,
TED RENAULT
Customer Service Manager

*To a consumer who has not sent payment with her order, as required, from a bicycle manufacturer (*NOTE: *In this letter, the writer is careful to justify a relatively inconvenient policy by explaining its value to the customer—a strategy that will help motivate customer compliance with the policy.):*

Dear Mrs. Vito,

Thank you for your November 17 order for Bikalot's Water Buffalo bicycle seat, model #77WB-2. It is a great value, and one reason we are able to offer it at such a low price is that we have a policy of shipping only orders that are prepaid. This results in a savings for us that we can pass along to our customers like you.

We have reserved your Bikalot Water Buffalo bicycle seat and will send it to you as soon as we receive your check or money order (no cash, please) for <u>$49.60,</u> which includes the seat price of $45.50, plus a $4.10 shipping charge. Please make your check or money order payable to "Bikalot."

We appreciate your choosing Bikalot.

> Yours truly,
> DAVID MEISTERLICH
> Director of Shipping

To a charity group seeking a special deal on a night that it can't be offered, from a theater manager (NOTE: *In this type of letter, the writer doesn't need to explain why he or she isn't granting a special request. A simple "I'm sorry" is sufficient. In the specific letter that appears below, the writer is able to offer alternatives.*):

Dear Mr. Triquet,

Thank you for writing Stratford Theater to request a block of 50 *Macbeth* tickets for Friday night, July 9, at a charitable discount of 50 percent. We are honored that United Fund chose a Stratford production.

I regret that we can offer only 50 full-price seats, scattered throughout the audience in small groups, for the night of Friday, July 9. We can, however, offer a block of 50 seats at a 50 percent discount for the following nights: Wednesday, July 7; Thursday, July 8; Sunday, July 11; Tuesday, July 13; and Thursday, July 15.

I will hold all these options open for you until May 15, so that you can choose the date that is most convenient for you. After May 15, these options may or may not still be available, depending on box office demand.

I sincerely hope Stratford Theater can help make an evening of *Macbeth* possible for clients of your fine organization.

> Very truly yours,
> MARY CHIN
> Manager

RESPONSES TO RESERVATIONS

To a tourist, from a resort hotel (NOTE: *Appearing below is a letter written to confirm that the reservation* can *be made as requested. Appearing after that are two other versions of the same letter: one in which the reservation* can *be made* with a slight change, *and one in which the reservation* can*not be made.):*

Dear Mr. Yarby,

Thank you for making Trillmore Arms part of your travel plans. We have received your deposit of $92.00 and are reserving a double room in your name for three nights: from Friday, August 2, through Sunday, August 4. As requested, the room is smoke-free and contains two full-size beds. Parking is available in our lot in back of the hotel.

It is Trillmore Arms' policy to hold reservations until 10 p.m. on the arrival date. However, if you will be arriving at a later time, please notify us and we will extend this deadline accordingly. Checkout time is 12 noon on the date of departure, but we have storage facilities for luggage if you'd like to remain in the area past 12 noon.

All of us at Trillmore Arms look forward to serving you. Please let me know if there's anything further we can do to make your stay as comfortable as possible.

> Very truly yours,
> CHRIS O'BRIEN
> Reservations Manager

To a tourist, from a resort hotel that can *make the requested reservation* with a slight change (NOTE: *In this type of letter, first state what you* can *offer, then state what you* can*not offer.):*

Dear Mr. Yarby,

Thank you for your interest in staying at Trillmore Arms and for sending us a deposit check of $92.00. For the three nights on which you requested accommodation—Friday, August 2, through Sunday, August 4—we can offer you two choices:

- a double room, smoke-free, with one full-size bed for all three nights (at $80.00 per night); or

- a double room, smoke-free, with one full-size bed for Friday night (at $80.00), and another double room, smoke-free, with two full-size beds for both Saturday and Sunday nights (at $92.00 per night).

I regret very much that a double room with two full-size beds for all three nights, as you requested, is not available due to previous reservations. This is true for smoke-free rooms as well as smoking rooms.

I sincerely hope that we at Trillmore Arms will have the opportunity to serve you. I will hold your deposit check until I hear from you.

Very truly yours,
CHRIS O'BRIEN
Reservations Manager

*To a tourist, from a resort hotel that can*not *make the requested reservation:*

Dear Mr. Yarby,

Thank you for your interest in staying at Trillmore Arms and for sending us your $92.00 deposit check for three nights: August 2 through 4. I regret very much that no rooms are available for these dates due to previous reservations, nor do we have any rooms available for the rest of August or for the first week of September. Therefore, I am returning your deposit check.

Trillmore Arms does currently have rooms available from September 8 through October 31, and we would welcome the opportunity to serve you.

Please contact me at your earliest convenience if you would like to make a reservation during this time period or at any time during the future. July and August dates are very popular, so it is best to reserve no later than the previous March.

Our best wishes to you for a happy summer.

Very truly yours,
CHRIS O'BRIEN
Reservations Manager

ELEVEN

Letters of Complaint and Responses

IF YOU HAVE A COMPLAINT regarding a product or a service, it's always advisable to write a letter about it to the company that is responsible for the product or service, even if you have already spoken in person or by telephone to a company representative. A letter of complaint functions as a permanent record and reminder of your grievance; and if it is properly written, it can help ensure that you don't experience future problems relating to that same complaint or that same company.

LETTERS OF COMPLAINT

Here are guidelines for writing an effective letter of complaint:

- If possible and reasonably convenient, address your complaint to a specific person rather than to a company or a title. Try telephoning the company switchboard and asking for an appropriate name (you don't have to talk with the person him- or herself). A request made to a specific individual is more likely to receive prompt and courteous attention. If you can't conveniently identify a name, use an appropriate-sounding title (e.g., "Customer Service Manager").
- Be firm, direct, and concise in your letter, without being nasty or argumentative. You are more likely to inspire satisfactory action

on your behalf by being calm and professional than you are by venting your anger.

In cases where the company has repeatedly given grounds for complaint or the incident under complaint has already caused or threatened a loss of property, credit, or reputation, you have a right to use especially strong language. However, you should still avoid undignified tirades or emotional outpourings (see "Erroneous Bill" below for a positive example of this type of letter).

• In the first paragraph of your letter, state the nature of your complaint clearly and include all the details that the reader might need to know to process your complaint (e.g., date of purchase; order number; brand name, model number, and price of product).

• After communicating the above-mentioned information, state clearly what you expect the reader to do in response to your complaint.

Appearing below are sample letters of complaint that follow the guidelines above. These letters cover a variety of common complaint situations. For responses to each of these letters, in order, see the section "Responses to Letters of Complaint," beginning on page 147.

RECEIPT OF DEFECTIVE PRODUCT

To an out-of-state vendor for whom no specific employee's name was readily available, from a mail-order customer (NOTE: *In this type of situation, it is generally better* not *to return the actual product unless specifically requested to do so, in which case postage should be paid for, or reimbursed by, the vendor.*):

Dear Customer Service Manager:

The Henley sweater I ordered from you on April 22 (order #4252: cobalt blue, medium, model C-34) was defective upon arrival, with a number of unsightly unravelings on the left sleeve. Please send me a replacement sweater of the exact same model, size, and color that is not defective, or advise me about what to do, as soon as possible.

Yours truly,

ANN FORRESTAL

To an out-of-state vendor for whom no specific employee's name was readily available, from a customer:

Dear Customer Service Manager:

On May 6, I received a Kaylord ventilation fan, model #23K, that I had ordered from Lincoln Supply (order #18822). Every time I've run the fan, it has buzzed loudly and erratically throughout its operation. The fan is clearly defective and, because of the noise it makes, unusable. Please send me a replacement fan in good working order as soon as possible.

Sincerely,

RITA PILLSWORTH

DELIVERY OF WRONG PRODUCT

To the shipping department of a hardware manufacturer, for whom no specific name was readily available, from a customer who is not willing to wait long or to accept a substitute product (NOTE: In this type of situation it is generally better not to return the actual product unless specifically requested to do so, in which case the vendor should arrange for pickup or mailing expenses.):

Dear Shipping Department Manager:

On September 11, 1993, I ordered an Acme Tool Case, model #5557-4-81 (order #3217) and enclosed payment for $156.35 (check #288). Today, your truck delivered a tool case labeled "Handy Helper's Tool Case," which does not resemble the one I ordered.

Please send me the tool case I ordered by October 31, or else refund my money.

Sincerely,

JOE KASHUKO

Overdue Delivery

To a vendor, for whom a specific name was not readily available, from a customer:

Dear Customer Service Manager:

On July 18, 1993, I purchased two gross of St. George golf balls from Hole-in-One, Inc. (order #5449), at which time I was assured delivery within two weeks. It is now almost a month later, and I have not received my order.

Please let me know immediately when I may expect receipt.

Sincerely yours,
KYLE MACDONALD

Dissatisfaction with Product

*To the vendor's customer service manager, from a customer who simply does not like the product and is entitled to return it (*NOTE: *In this type of situation, it is generally better to return the product, asking for a refund of the return postage, unless otherwise directed by vendor policy or the guarantee.):*

Dear Mr. Fassinger,

Under the conditions of my 30-day guarantee, I am returning the Impacto shredder I purchased on April 16, 1994, for $116.72 (photocopy of receipt enclosed). It does not produce the kind of fine, uniform-quality mulch that I need to get from hardwood branches 1½ inches thick or less. Instead, it produces large amounts of overly big chunks or dust.

Please refund my purchase payment of $116.72, along with the postage I paid for the return of the shredder, as soon as possible.

Yours truly,
MARGARET WONG

To the vendor's customer service manager, from a customer who be-lieves that the product was misrepresented and who does not possess a refund guarantee:

Dear Ms. Robinson,

I am returning the Gingko clock radio that I purchased from your store on October 20, 1994, for $89.51 (photocopy of receipt enclosed). The 10-minute snooze alarm feature does not, in fact, respond to "normal-volume" voice command within 10 feet, as the outside of the box says it does. Using my voice, I can turn off the radio only by shouting directly into the unit microphone from a distance no greater than six inches.

Since the clock radio does not perform as indicated by the manufacturer, I expect a full and immediate refund of $89.51, plus the postage I paid for return of the radio.

Sincerely,
Martin Peldorff

Erroneous Bill

To a department store manager, from a long-standing customer who is confident that the store has made a mistake and who is, appropriately, very angry:

Dear Mr. Niebuhr,

I am very upset at having received a bill from Sheeton's Department Store for $1,180.36 (photocopy enclosed), with the statement that my account will be turned over to a collection agency if it is not paid in full within 10 days. In fact, I have no outstanding debt with Sheeton's Department Store, nor have I ever owed this amount.

I demand an immediate explanation for your insulting letter. I have been a customer in good standing with Sheeton's Department Store for 10 years, and I deserve better treatment.

Sincerely,
Lorraine Pauling

BILLING MISUNDERSTANDING

To an electrician, from a customer who disagrees with the specific charges:

Dear Mr. Hefner,

I have received your August 13 bill for $615.00 (account #7219). I am not in agreement with one of the charges listed on that bill, so I am withholding payment until we can resolve the matter between us.

Per your original estimate of the electrical work to be done on the addition to my house, we agreed to a total cost of $550, based on using #36 copper piping throughout: a total cost for piping of $175. In your August 13 bill, you charged me $240 for more expensive #42 copper piping. As I was never informed of the change in piping, and as we agreed to use #36 copper piping, I feel it is not fair to charge me an additional $65, above the cost of the estimate.

Please resubmit a bill that accords with the total cost to which we originally agreed, $550, and I will reimburse you promptly. I am very satisfied with your work, and I don't want this misunderstanding to stand in the way of any future business between us.

Very truly yours,
PATRICK WASHINGTON

RETURNED CHECK

To a bank manager, regarding a check that was bounced due to an error on the bank's part:

Dear Mr. Tremont,

I am writing to you concerning a serious error made by Allied Bank regarding my checking account—one that disturbs me a great deal. American Drain Company has notified me that your bank returned my February 16 check to them for $750.00 (#663) marked "insufficient funds." In fact, I had over $5,000.00 in my checking account at that time. I enclose a photocopy of the check and of my most recent checking account statement, covering this time period.

I have instructed American Drain Company to redeposit my check #663, and I expect your bank to cash it. Furthermore, I expect you to write an apology to me and to the American Drain Company (address below) for the inconvenience we've been caused.

Very truly yours,
AARON MENDENHALL

cc: American Drain Company
1772 Van Seeler Avenue
Utica, NY 13501

DISSATISFACTION WITH SERVICE

To a business machine company regarding an unsatisfactory representative:

Dear Mr. Oatley,

I am writing to inform you that I am very dissatisfied with Harley St. Clair, the PBM representative who currently serves my company, Dateline Enterprises. Please assign another representative to our account, effective immediately.

In repeated, unsolicited conversations with me and my associates, Mr. St. Clair has employed unprofessional language and inappropriately aggressive selling techniques in an effort to get us to purchase additional PBM equipment or services. I am not averse to considering additional purchases, but I am definitely not responsive to suggestions that I am, as Mr. St. Clair once stated, "a fool" who is "sitting back and letting other companies take the lead" if I do not do as he says. Nor can I tolerate any account representative contacting other people in my company without first securing my consent, as all business machine purchase, repair, and maintenance decisions fall within my personal area of responsibility.

Aside from this unfortunate situation, I have enjoyed good relations with PBM customer service personnel, so I assume that the behavior I have described is not, in fact, characteristic of your organization. I would appreciate your letting me know as soon as possible who our new representative will be.

Sincerely yours,
EVELYN METCALF

Repeatedly Poor Service on a Contract

*To a caterer, with whom the writer, a vineyard owner, has a yearly renewable contract engaging the caterer to provide banquet services once a week and on special occasions (*NOTE: *The writer's lawyer is sent a copy of this letter for legal purposes, since the letter summarizes the relatively detailed history of the situation.):*

Dear Ms. Underhill,

Numerous times during the four months that have passed since I signed my year-long contract with Underhill Catering, I have had to complain to you about poor service. In each case, you apologized and promised to improve. Although some improvement was observable immediately following each complaint, the overall quality of service has continued to be inconsistent and subject to negative comments from my customers.

Here is an up-to-date summary of the poor service conditions that I've brought to your attention over the last four months, either by letter, telephone, or face-to-face conversation:

- *Dirty linen*
  Our contract states that you will provide clean, spot-free linen for each engagement and that dirtied linen will be replaced promptly during each engagement. Nevertheless, several times I have had to point out to you that tablecloths with highly visible stains were put on the tables by your staff. Each time you assured me that this would not happen again, but that did not turn out to be my experience.
- *Cold food*
  Our contract states that heated food will not be allowed to cool before serving, and yet, as I have informed you, guests have complained on several occasions that the food they were served was unpalatably cold. The latest complaint occurred after you said that food would "never be allowed to cool again."
- *Rude remarks*
  Our contract states that your cooking, serving, and cleanup staff members are to be courteous to guests, are not to engage guests in unsolicited conversation, and are not to converse among themselves in front of guests. Nevertheless, all of these conditions have been violated several times, including two incidents that you

yourself witnessed, when staff members speaking profanities were overheard by several guests. My own recent on-site observations do not satisfy me that sufficient measures have been taken to prevent future incidents of this nature.

I am reluctant to cancel my contract with you. However, I will be forced to do so, under the conditions outlined in paragraph 8, unless there is a substantial and lasting improvement in service, particularly in the areas I have just mentioned.

If necessary, I am willing to meet with you to discuss this situation further. Otherwise, I expect a signed letter from you as soon as possible assuring me that you will prevent any recurrence of the causes for complaint outlined in this letter, and that your services in the future will conform to the provisions stated in our contract.

Sincerely,
PAUL LEGRANDE

cc: Phyllis Corotte, Esq.
Attorney-at-Law

SHIPMENT OF WRONG ORDER

To the supplier, from a new customer who has already talked with the supplier on the phone:

Dear Mrs. Halliburton,

This letter confirms our telephone conversation today regarding Milton Furniture's error in filling my order #10032. It also informs you of further consequences of that error.

To reiterate, I placed an order with you for 50 folding chairs, model #4995, on June 12, 1993. At that time, I specified that I wanted this order to consist of 15 red chairs, 15 blue chairs, and 20 white chairs, to satisfy existing customer requests. Today, I telephoned you to let you know that I received 50 white chairs and no red or blue chairs. You agreed to send me 15 blue chairs and 15 red chairs by July 8 and to arrange for pickup of the 30 surplus white chairs.

Since that conversation, I spoke with the customers who ordered the blue and red chairs. They were very upset about not being able to have the specific chairs they ordered in time for scheduled July 4 events. As a result, I was compelled to sell them the white chairs instead at a discount of 20 percent a chair, resulting in a total loss to me of $240. Since the original mistake was yours, I am hoping that you will reduce my bill for the order by the same amount.

I admire your products, and I'd like to be able to rely on your integrity and good service in the future. Please advise me as soon as possible of your decision in this particular matter and of what you intend to do to prevent similar errors in the future.

Very truly yours,
CLIFF GARDINER

SHIPMENT OF POOR-QUALITY PRODUCT

To the representative of a supplier, from a client who is on friendly terms:

Dear Beth,

I have never before had a complaint about one of your products, but I'm afraid I do now. Several customers have returned the Holden 10 × 13″ clasp envelopes, model X6645, which I ordered on June 3, 1994 (order #225), saying that the mucilage on the envelope flap does not become sufficiently sticky when moistened. I have also found this to be true myself.

Would you please check out this situation personally, Beth, and determine whether my receipt of this substandard batch was an accident or, instead, the result of a change in production quality? If it was an accident, I'm willing to stay with the Holden brand. Otherwise, I will have to shift brands.

Meanwhile, I'm sending back the remaining 82 boxes from this order and requesting credit for the full order of 100 boxes. Random sampling has convinced me that all boxes are affected and that I must refer customers elsewhere for 10 × 13″ clasp envelopes rather than risk their displeasure by selling them an inferior product.

Thank you for your prompt attention to this matter, Beth. I expect to hear from you within the week.

Best wishes,
ROGER

RESPONSES TO LETTERS OF COMPLAINT

When responding to a letter of complaint, it is usually best to be as accommodating and as courteous as possible. Always remember that your desired objective is to defuse the recipient's anger and to retain him or her as a satisfied customer or client. Here are other important guidelines:

- In the first paragraph of your letter, you should restate the complaint, in terms that are the least damaging to you, as well as all pertinent information that will assist the reader to recall the complaint (e.g., date of purchase; order number; brand name, model number, and price of product).
- After communicating the above-mentioned information, you should clearly and concisely state the action you are going to take in response to the complaint. As much as possible, this should involve fulfilling the specific requests of the complainer.
- Admit any error that your company may have made, but avoid being defensive or deprecating your company. Unless specifically requested to do so, you don't have to offer explanations, and you should never offer excuses (there being no excuse, from the complainer's perspective, for mistakes).
- If you have been falsely accused, or if you cannot, for good reason, honor the complainer's request, then you should explain the situation as clearly, concisely, and tactfully as possible. If at all possible, you should then offer to do something appropriately conciliatory for the complainer, even if it hasn't been specifically requested (see "Billing Misunderstanding" below for a positive example of this kind of letter).
- Always apologize for the inconvenience caused by the complaint, and express your hopes for a good business relationship in the future.

Appearing below are sample response letters that follow the guidelines above. For the original letter of complaint corresponding to each of these response letters, in order, see the section "Letters of Complaint," beginning on page 137.

RECEIPT OF DEFECTIVE PRODUCT

To a mail-order customer from out of state, who received a sweater with unravelings:

Dear Ms. Forrestal,

I was very sorry to learn that the Henley sweater you ordered was defective upon arrival. A replacement sweater in good condition (cobalt blue, medium, model C-34) is being sent to you today, without charge. It should arrive within 10 days.

We sincerely regret the inconvenience this has caused you.

Sincerely,
MARK DUMONT
Director of Customer Service

To a customer who received a malfunctioning ventilation fan but did not return it (store policy does not demand return, but return is appreciated):

Dear Ms. Pillsworth,

Thank you for your June 11 letter, informing us of the noise problem you were having with your Kaylord ventilation fan (model #23K). You were right to conclude that the fan must be defective, since Kaylord fans are well known for running quietly and unobtrusively. We are sending you a free replacement fan, which you should receive within two weeks.

We would greatly appreciate it if you would return the defective fan so that we can alert the manufacturer to the specific problem involved. We will, of course, reimburse you for the postage.

Please accept our apology for the delay and trouble you've experienced. Customers like you are valuable to us, and I hope you will continue to shop at Lincoln Supply.

Very truly yours,
RUDOLPH MUELLER
Customer Service Manager

DELIVERY OF WRONG PRODUCT

To a customer who did not return the product and who wanted a replacement by a certain date or else a refund (store policy demands return):

Dear Mr. Kashuko,

Thank you for your letter of September 28, informing us that you received the Handy Helper's Tool Case instead of the Acme Tool Case you ordered. Unfortunately, we are unable to arrange for delivery of the Acme Tool Case by October 31 as you requested. Therefore, we are prepared to refund your $156.35, plus any shipping expenses, as soon as the Handy Helper's Tool Case is returned to us.

The Acme Tool Case was taken out of production before your order could be filled. It was replaced in the Builtmore product line by the Handy Helper's Tool Case, which is sold for $174.00, but which we sent to you at no additional charge. I sincerely regret that you were not informed of the substitution in a more direct and timely manner.

We think that the Handy Helper's Tool Case is an excellent product. If you want, you may keep it instead of applying for a refund, or you may purchase it at a later date for the same price that you originally paid for the Acme Tool Case ($156.35).

Please accept my personal apology for the confusion and inconvenience that you've been caused.

Yours truly,
RAPHAEL FUENTES
Manager, Shipping Department

OVERDUE DELIVERY

To a customer who has not received his order two weeks after delivery was expected:

Dear Mr. MacDonald,

I very much regret the delay you've experienced in receiving the two gross of golf balls you purchased from Hole-in-One, Inc. Today,

I have ordered a rush shipment to you, which should arrive at your address no later than August 25.

Thank you for bringing this matter to our attention. I assure you that such delays are not typical of the service we provide, nor are they acceptable to us. Please give us the opportunity to serve you better in the future.

Sincerely,
DEENA DEVICTOR
Public Relations Manager

DISSATISFACTION WITH PRODUCT

To a customer who is returning the product, as entitled, because she doesn't like it (store policy dictates that refunds be made as store credit, rather than cash or check):

Dear Ms. Wong,

I am sorry that the Impacto shredder that you purchased from Maximo Merchant Mart did not produce the kind of mulch you need. Thank you for returning it. Because you are covered by our 30-day guarantee policy, I am enclosing a credit voucher for $126.50, which includes the $116.72 purchase price and the $9.78 cost of postage.

I am also enclosing brochures that describe other shredders we sell at Maximo Merchant Mart. I sincerely hope that you will return to us to purchase the type of shredder that best suits your needs. Our sales staff will help you to make the right choice based on your particular situation.

Thank you for shopping with us.

Very truly yours,
HOWARD FASSINGER
Sales Manager

To a customer who is returning merchandise that is not covered by a guarantee, claiming that the product was misrepresented. (NOTE: In such cases, it is generally better not to challenge or to confirm the customer's specific claim, but simply to acknowledge that the product doesn't work

*and to act accordingly. Otherwise, you risk greater business loss by alien-
ating the customer and generating ill will.):*

Dear Mr. Peldorff:
We are sorry that the Gingko clock radio that you purchased at
Appliance City was defective. Thank you for returning it and calling
this matter to our attention. Enclosed is our refund check for $95.61
($89.51 price, plus $6.10 return postage).
We value customers like you who care about quality, and hope
that you will continue to give Appliance City the benefit of serving
you.

Sincerely,
GINGER ROBINSON
Account Executive

ERRONEOUS BILL

*To a customer who was irate because she received the wrong bill and
who demanded an explanation, from the vendor who sent the bill. (NOTE:
In this type of situation, when a customer has demanded an explanation,
the vendor should be sure to offer one.)*

Dear Ms. Pauling,
Please accept our deepest apologies for having sent you the wrong
bill for $1,180.36. You are correct in stating that you had no
outstanding debt with Sheeton's Department Store at the time, and I
can imagine how bewildered and upset you must have been to
receive that bill.
I have personally investigated the matter and have determined that
it was the result of a freak computer malfunction that substituted
your account number for another account number. Our computer
records are now correct, and I can assure you that you won't
experience any further difficulties relating to this unfortunate error.
You will receive a correct revised statement within 10 days.
We regret very much the concern and inconvenience this mistake
has caused you. Sheeton's Department Store appreciates your many
years of loyalty and wants to do everything possible to keep you

happy with the products and services we offer. Please contact me directly if you ever need assistance again.

Thank you for informing us promptly about this situation.

Very truly yours,
TERRY NIEBUHR
General Manager

BILLING MISUNDERSTANDING

To a customer who disagrees with a billing charge (NOTE: *The following example reflects a situation in which the customer is right to complain; the example after that, responding to the same letter, reflects a situation in which the customer is mistaken.*):

Dear Mr. Washington,

Thank you for your letter of August 15, noting the discrepancy between our July 1 estimate of $550 for electrical work on your addition and our August 13 bill of $615. You are correct in stating that you should not be charged for the difference between these two amounts. Attached is a revised bill, in which you are credited for the difference and obligated to pay no more than the amount of the original estimate ($550).

As you pointed out, the discrepancy between the July 1 estimate and the August 13 bill was due to the fact that #42 copper piping was used, at a cost of $240, rather than the #36 copper piping indicated on the estimate, which would have cost $175. I made the decision to substitute the thicker #42 piping for the #36 piping during the excavation itself.

At that time I determined that the water and soil in the area where the piping needed to be laid were more acidic and more subject to freezing than was previously apparent, and that you would be better served if I used the thicker piping. However, I did not secure your written consent to make this substitution as I should have, according to the conditions expressed in the original estimate.

I apologize for the trouble that this incident has caused you. Thank you for expressing your satisfaction with our work, and please call upon us for any future needs.

Sincerely,
JERRY HEFNER
General Contractor

To the same customer as above, reflecting a situation in which the customer is mistaken:

Dear Mr. Washington,

Thank you for your letter of August 15, noting the discrepancy between our July 1 estimate of $550 for electrical work on your addition and our August 13 bill of $615. I believe that the August 13 bill of $615 is a fair one, and it remains my charge for the work done on your addition.

As you pointed out, that discrepancy between the July 1 estimate and the August 13 bill was due to the fact that #42 copper piping was used at a cost of $240, rather than the #36 copper piping indicated on the estimate, which would have cost $175. If you will recall, we discussed this matter during the excavation itself.

At that time I told you that the water and soil in the areas where the piping needed to be laid were more acidic and more subject to freezing than was previously apparent, and that you would be better served if I substituted the thicker #42 piping for the #36 piping. You agreed to the substitution and authorized me to make it.

Estimates are, by nature, subject to change according to discoveries that are made and incidents that occur during the work in progress. As our estimate form states (paragraph #4), "Any change resulting in a higher cost than the final cost expressed in this estimate should be brought to the attention of the client prior to being incurred, and should not be incurred without the client's verbal consent." The conversation in which I received your verbal consent to the change in piping was one of many we had over the course of the construction, so it is certainly possible that you may have forgotten it by the time you received my bill.

I very much regret this misunderstanding. I, too, enjoyed our working relationship and would welcome the chance to collaborate again. If you would like to arrange for an extension of the payment due date or a time-payment plan, please don't hesitate to call.

Sincerely,
JERRY HEFNER
General Contractor

Returned Check

To a customer, regarding a check that was bounced due to an error on the bank's part:

Dear Mr. Mendenhall,

Regarding your letter of March 14, you are correct in stating that your Allied Bank check #663, in the amount of $750.00, was erroneously returned to the American Drain Company on February 17 marked "insufficient funds." In fact, you did have sufficient funds in your account at that time, and our computer made a rare and unfortunate error in reporting that you did not. Your check should have been honored on receipt.

Our records show that American Drain Company has not yet redeposited your check. If they have not redeposited it by the time they receive their copy of this letter, I am asking them to do so as soon as they wish. In either case, I have already made sure that there will be no further problems. You are a valued customer who has always been in good standing with Allied Bank.

I sincerely regret the inconvenience this error has caused you and the American Drain Company. Thank you for calling it to our attention so efficiently, and please accept our sincere apologies.

Yours truly,
Aaron Mendenhall
Account Manager

cc: American Drain Company

Dissatisfaction with Service

*To a customer who complained regarding an unsatisfactory representative, from the company who assigned the representative (*NOTE: *For a similar letter that introduces a new representative, but is* not *responding to a complaint, see page 176.):*

Dear Ms. Metcalf,

I sincerely regret that you were not satisfied with the conduct of our PBM representative, Mr. Harley St. Clair. You were right to bring this matter to our attention. Effective immediately, Mr. Keith

Wells replaces Mr. St. Clair on your account. He will be calling you soon to arrange a mutually convenient opportunity to introduce himself.

Mr. Wells is one of our most highly regarded representatives. He has served valued PBM customers effectively and graciously for eight years. I am confident that you will find him very professional in his conduct, as well as very responsive to your purchase, repair, and maintenance needs.

Thank you for saying that you have enjoyed good relations with PBM customer service personnel, apart from this particular situation. Outstanding customer service is a priority at PBM, and we join you in refusing to tolerate anything less.

Sincerely,
ROBERT OATLEY
Division Service Manager

REPEATEDLY POOR SERVICE ON A CONTRACT

To a vineyard owner who has written a list of complaints, and who has threatened to cancel a yearly renewable contract, from a caterer (NOTE: *In the face of strong criticism about the quality of one's service, it is best to be as polite and compliant as possible without sacrificing one's dignity. This involves taking extra pains to reflect the client's language and thereby demonstrate that he or she has been heard. It also involves subtly encouraging the client to make any future complaints more constructively and with greater equanimity. For a closer look at how this is done, compare this letter with the original complaint letter, which appears on page 144.)*

Dear Mr. LeGrande,

In response to your October 11 letter, I am writing to express my deep regret for the situations that have given you cause to complain about Underhill Catering's services. I assure you that my staff and I will work diligently to prevent any recurrence of these causes, and that future services will conform to the provisions stated in our contract.

We will give special attention to the issues raised in your letter:

* Clean linen

  As our contract states, we will provide clean, spot-free linen for each engagement, and replace dirtied linen as soon as possible. We recognize that it is our responsibility to be vigilant in this matter, but we would also welcome you or your associates bringing to our attention any dirty linen that you notice.

- Warm food

  As our contract states, heated food will not be allowed to cool before serving. Please do not hesitate to let us know whenever served food is cool, or whenever you have special reason to suspect that the food might become too cool to be served.

- Courtesy

  As our contract states, all of our staff members will be courteous to guests, will not engage guests in unsolicited conversation, and will not converse among themselves in front of guests. If you should observe any behavior that you find questionable, we would appreciate your telling us.

We are very honored to be your caterer, and we sincerely hope you will accept our apologies for the concerns that you have experienced. Thank you for your patience and understanding.

Very truly yours,

PATRICIA UNDERHILL

President, Underhill Catering

SHIPMENT OF WRONG ORDER

To a new customer whose order for chairs was misfilled and who is requesting a discount, from a furniture supplier (NOTE: *In this type of situation, the supplier, who is responsible for the original mistake, should agree to meet all reasonable demands made by the client relating to that mistake.*)

Dear Mr. Gardiner,

Thank you for your letter of July 3, regarding the erroneous shipment to you of 30 white #4995 chairs, rather than 15 red and 15 blue chairs. We regret very much the trouble this error has caused you. As a result, we are reducing your bill for order #10032 by $240, as you requested. We are also canceling the shipment of 15 red chairs and 15 blue chairs that was meant to replace the 30 surplus white chairs, which you have already sold.

We appreciate your kind words regarding our products, and look forward to providing you with better service in the future. Please feel free to contact me directly if you have any questions or comments regarding your orders from Milton Furniture.

Sincerely,
LEE HALLIBURTON
Account Manager

SHIPMENT OF POOR-QUALITY PRODUCT

To a customer, from a supplier who is on friendly terms:

Dear Roger,

I received your letter of June 30 about the Holden 10 × 13″ clasp envelopes you ordered (order #225). You are right about the mucilage not being dependably sticky when moistened, as I found out in my own sample lickings from the same batch number. You will, of course, receive credit for the full order of 100 boxes.

The Holden Company assures me that the mucilage problem in this particular batch of envelopes was the result of a production or shipping accident and does not reflect any change in ingredients or quality standards, which, as you know, are unexcelled in the industry. I'm convinced that you can rely on them for future orders, and I'm prepared to make your next order a "rush" order, with no additional shipping charge, whenever you choose to place it.

I'm very sorry about the trouble you've had with this, Roger. Thanks for being so understanding.

Sincerely,
BETH

TWELVE

Letters of Reference, Commendation, and Opinion

COMMON OCCASIONS that call for writing a business letter assessing someone you know include the following:

- A current or former employee, student, or associate asks you to write to a specific potential employer.
- A current or former employee, student, or associate asks you to write a general "to-whom-it-may-concern" letter that he or she can show to potential employers.
- Someone who is interviewing applicants asks you to write a letter about one of your former employees, students, or associates whom he or she is considering for a position.
- You would like to reward someone for good performance in a business situation by calling that performance to the attention of his or her superior. (NOTE: For thanking someone directly, a more informal situation, see chapter 5, "Thank-you Notes and Letters." For complaining about someone's performance in a business situation, see chapter 11, "Letters of Complaint and Responses.")
- You would like to recommend someone for membership in an organization.

Here are general guidelines applying to letters of reference and commendation:

- When first mentioning the subject of the letter (the person being described), use his or her *full* name. Thereafter, whenever you refer to the subject by name, always use the *last* name with an appropriate title (e.g., "Dr.," "Mr.," or "Ms."), never the first name alone.

  For the first reference to the subject within each paragraph after the first paragraph, it is common practice to use the title and last name instead of "he" or "she." For the remaining references within each paragraph, use "he" or "she."

- In addition to announcing the subject and main purpose of your letter in the first paragraph, be sure to identify your "official" relationship with the subject (e.g., "supervisor," "adviser," or "associate") and the time period of that relationship.

- Be relatively brief and general in your remarks. One page covering the subject's major achievements, qualities, and capabilities is usually sufficient for the recipient's purposes; at the same time it helps prevent you from inadvertently saying something inappropriate, boring the reader, or lapsing into hyperbole. If, however, the person requesting the letter asks you to address certain issues in detail, then feel free to do so.

- If you're writing to dispose the reader favorably toward your subject, and you're reasonably sure what kinds of achievements, qualities, and skills are most likely to interest your reader, then focus on them in your discussion. Otherwise, stick to discussing the achievements, qualities, and skills that most impressed you.

- Be honest in your letter. If you can wholeheartedly recommend your subject, then of course you'll want to put him or her in the most positive light possible. However, if you feel obligated to say negative things about your subject, then do so. Always remember that a letter of reference affects the reputation of its writer as well as its subject, and you don't want to risk being considered untrustworthy.

  When you do have negative things to say about your subject, try to be as positive as you can be in the letter as a whole—for example, by calling primary attention to the subject's good points, or by using temperate rather than strong language to make critical remarks. Also, indicate to the reader in your closing that you expect your remarks to be kept confidential.

RECOMMENDATIONS: POSITIVE AND NEGATIVE

The following model letters reflect different situations involving letters of reference or commendation:

To a company manager at Pacer & Pacer checking out a reference, from the job seeker's current boss at Bodell Advertising Agency, who is able to give an unqualified recommendation:

Dear Mr. Glass,

Thank you for your September 30 inquiry regarding Ms. Noreen Watson's job qualifications. As the president of Bodell Advertising Agency and Ms. Watson's employer since July 22, 1992, I am happy to report that Ms. Watson is a gifted designer, a good team player, and a very dedicated and productive employee. She would definitely be an asset to your organization.

Ms. Watson began at Bodell Advertising as an administrative assistant. In that capacity, she was extremely proficient in data processing, production scheduling, and reorganizing office files and procedural policies. Thanks to her own hard work and initiative, and to commercial art courses that she took on her own behalf at St. Oland College's night school, she progressed to the job of assistant designer within 18 months. After just six months in that position, her innovative and popular work led me to promote her to the job of designer, in which she consults directly with client companies and independent contractors to create and implement advertising campaigns in all media. She has consistently performed her job with skill, enthusiasm, and success.

I will be sorry to see Ms. Watson leave Bodell Advertising Agency, but at the same time I understand her wish to pursue other career opportunities besides the ones that we can presently offer her. Pacer & Pacer would be fortunate, indeed, to have her. Please don't hesitate to contact me if I can offer any other information.

Sincerely yours,
WILLIAM BODELL
President

To a prospective first-time employer checking out a reference, from the job seeker's college adviser, who is able to give an unqualified recommendation:

Dear Mr. Takiya,

In response to your August 20 letter, I am very glad to write on behalf Mr. Allen Kennedy, whom you are considering for a management trainee position at Cloverdale, Inc. I was Mr. Kennedy's faculty adviser during his four years at Merrimee State University, where he was awarded a bachelor of arts degree in language and literature last June.

Mr. Kennedy is an intelligent, resourceful, and energetic man, who favorably impressed all of his teachers at Merrimee and who earned great respect, admiration, and popularity among his student peers. While maintaining a high academic average throughout his undergraduate career, he also became constructively involved in numerous extracurricular activities, including Pen & Pencil (the literary club), The *Merrimmee Spectator* (the campus newspaper, of which he was editor during his senior year), and the Society of 1918 (a community service group). I am confident that his outstanding skills as a writer, speaker, worker, and leader will prove to be of great value to your organization.

Please feel free to contact me again if you need further information.

> Very truly yours,
> MICHAEL RUGGIERO (Dr.)
> Maitland Professor of Language

To a company executive at Kelzo Enterprises checking out a reference, from the job seeker's former boss at Ross Associates, who cannot give an unqualified recommendation (NOTE: *Another version of this letter, in which the writer is compelled to give a much more negative response, immediately follows this version.*):

Dear Ms. Garcia,

I am writing in response to your letter of March 6 regarding Mr. Tim Reardon, who is seeking a managerial position at Kelzo Enterprises. During the three years that Mr. Reardon was an assistant manager of production at Ross Associates under my supervision, November 1991 to November 1994, I generally found him to be very eager, hard-working, and effective. He takes his job duties quite seriously; and if you hire him, I am confident that you will find him an industrious and conscientious employee.

Regrettably, I must also say that Mr. Reardon's style of interacting with others during his years at Ross Associates would occasionally be brusk or insensitive, to the point where I needed to intervene to resolve conflicts. He is aware of this issue, and I believe he is quite likely to demonstrate more tact in a more responsible position, especially if he receives the benefit of training in interpersonal skills.

I hope you will give Mr. Reardon an opportunity not only to show you his excellent qualities as a performer, but also to grow into the outstanding manager he is capable of becoming.

Sincerely,
RUSSELL KIMBOLDT
Vice President, Production

*To a company executive at Kelzo Enterprises checking out a reference, from the job seeker's former boss at Ross Associates, who is compelled to give a very negative response (*NOTE: *Another version of this letter, in which the response is much less negative, appears directly above.)*

Dear Ms. Garcia,

I am writing in response to your letter of March 6 regarding Mr. Tim Reardon, who is seeking a managerial position at Kelzo Enterprises. For three years (November 1991 to November 1994), Mr. Reardon was an assistant manager of production at Ross Associates under my supervision. Regrettably, I cannot recommend him for the position he is seeking.

Although Mr. Reardon was a hard worker on an independent basis during his years at Ross Associates, he was consistently incapable of maintaining productive relationships with other employees. He frequently challenged my authority and behaved toward his peers and subordinates with arrogance, defiance, and a general lack of understanding and cooperativeness. This conduct, which more and more often required my supervisory attention, prevented him from advancing in his career at Ross Associates and, ultimately, led to our decision to terminate his employment.

Please consider my remarks as a courtesy to you, given my regard for your company and for the effort you are making to find a competent employee. I assume they will be kept confidential.

Sincerely,
RUSSELL KIMBOLDT
Vice President, Production

To whom it may concern, from an employer recommending a household employee (NOTE: *It is always better to address a letter of reference to a specific individual than to write a "to whom it may concern" letter. However, in a situation involving a household employee such as a domestic, nanny, or chauffeur—or any employee who is similarly subject to relocation and rapid job turnover—it is wise to give the employee a "to whom it may concern" letter. The employee can then keep it in his or her file as an all-purpose backup reference, just in case you are not easily available to write directly to a prospective employer.):*

To whom it may concern:

Ms. Theresa Jackson was employed by me as a maid from January 1989 to July 1994, at which time I moved from 1344 Ventour Avenue in Richmond, Virginia, to my present address in Colorado and no longer required her services. Ms. Jackson's duties during that time period included keeping the interior of my 11-room house clean and well maintained, laundering household linens and clothes for two adults and three children, receiving visitors and telephone calls, and supervising service personnel during house visits.

In all Ms. Jackson's assigned duties, and in the many additional duties that she undertook from time to time at my request or on her own initiative, she demonstrated great skill, efficiency, reliability, and professionalism. She was always a highly trusted and valued member of our household, whom I can recommend wholeheartedly as a domestic employee or household manager.

I would be glad to respond personally to any inquiries about Ms. Jackson's capabilities, accomplishments, and character.

Sincerely,
ROSEMARIE WARDEN (Mrs.)
72 Culver Road
Denver, Colorado 80221

To the office manager of Ridgely Savings and Loan Company, from the office manager of Providential Insurance Company, recommending a pest control service:

Dear Mr. Hwang,

I am writing in response to your April 17 letter asking my opinion of O'Dea Exterminators. I can recommend O'Dea very highly.

For eight years, Providential Insurance Company has relied on O'Dea, and O'Dea has lived up to its original promise to keep our 17-room office free of cockroaches, termites, ants, mice, and other common indoor pests. The O'Dea personnel are always prompt, well dressed, and polite, and they have never disturbed the normal course of business. In addition, their rates are quite reasonable compared with other, similar services I have investigated.

Please let me know if you need further information.

Best regards,
Yvette Lozada

To a company's vice president of sales and marketing, from a customer commending a representative of that company (NOTE: This type of letter, praising a company employee, is much more effective if it is addressed to a higher-ranking manager or executive in the company. The letter will then get passed down to the employee's boss, who will be all the more impressed that the letter received "higher" attention, and ultimately, to the employee him- or herself.):

Dear Mr. Lee,

I frequently shop at the main Fordacker store on Livingston Street, and I've always received prompt, courteous attention from your customer service personnel. On Saturday, August 15, however, Mark Rulimann, a representative in your sporting-goods section, was exceptionally helpful, and I wanted to write to you commending him.

That Saturday, my son Arthur and I consulted with Mr. Rulimann about buying free weights and exercise equipment for a home gym. Mr. Rulimann not only answered all our questions knowledgeably and thoughtfully, but he also took the time to help Arthur successfully try out some of the more complicated gear. I was very impressed with his sincere concern that we get the particular weights and equipment that would best suit our needs, and with his tact and skill in dealing with a very choosy fourteen-year-old.

My congratulations go to you on having such a good representative on your team! Please extend my thanks to Mr. Rulimann for making a difficult chore much easier.

Very truly yours,
ED STAVANGAR

To the president of a club, from a member proposing a new member:

Dear Mr. Sherwood,
I would like to propose Mr. Paul Kenilworth for membership in the Leader's Club. He is very enthusiastic about becoming more actively involved in community service, and I believe his intelligence, organizational talents, and good humor would make him an outstanding addition to our ranks.

Mr. Kenilworth has recently moved to Pittsburgh from Chicago, Illinois, where he was a sales manager for Dateco Office Products and a member of the Optimist Club and the Toastmaster's Club. He is currently district sales manager for Dateco in Pittsburgh. Since we worked together two months ago on a highly successful fund-raiser for Mountainview Hospital, he has been a good friend, whose character I respect and whose conduct I admire.

Please let me know if I may invite Mr. Kenilworth to a club meeting so that you and the membership can meet him.

Sincerely yours,
JOHN CAPRIA

LETTERS TO THE EDITOR

A "letter to the editor" is written in response to any item appearing in a newspaper or magazine: an article, an editorial, a column, a cartoon, or another letter to the editor. Most periodicals publish their own specific guidelines regarding letters to the editor in each issue, including such information as maximum letter length and how to identify yourself (e.g., they may want both your name and the name of your city or town and state; and they may not accept letters in which the name is withheld). In general, however, a letter to the editor should be relatively brief (no more than 300 words): not only to keep from boring the reader, but also to keep the editor from trimming the letter as he or she prefers (which is an editor's right).

Your letter to the editor should always be addressed "To the Editor," rather than to the author of the item to which you are responding, or to some other party. In the first paragraph of your letter to the editor, always be sure to identify the item to which you are responding by its title and date. If your letter as a whole represents a negative response to that item, remember that it's far more constructive to attack a particular *topic* or *opinion* than to attack a particular *person*.

Here are two models of letters to the editor: first, a letter representing a positive response, then a letter representing a negative response:

To a newspaper's "Letter to the Editor" feature, from a reader who is agreeing with, and adding to, a recent editorial opinion:

To the Editor:

Your March 24 editorial "Life and Death on Lake Charles" was correct in saying that there is an urgent need to improve boating safety in our local waters. I also agree that a major step in this direction would be the mandatory training and licensing of boaters. However, much more needs to be done. State and local boating agencies, private boating groups, insurance companies, and boat manufacturers and dealers must work actively together to prevent and minimize boating accidents, injuries, and deaths.

One way to do this is for all these interested parties to combine their resources and create a "Register of Accidents" for recreational boating. This register could set up authoritative criteria for evaluating boating accidents more carefully, so that specific hazards could be better understood and specific solutions to those hazards could be more effectively developed.

As a recreational boater who is concerned about accident prevention and reduction, I appeal to leaders in any and all of these groups to take the initiative in this "Register of Accidents" project.

The best chance we have of making our waters safer for boaters is for all knowledgeable parties to share their expertise.

MARVIN SEELEY
Horton, Nebraska

To a newspaper's "Letter to the Editor" feature, from a reader who vehemently disagrees with the writer of an article that recently appeared in the paper:

To the Editor:

In "One-Way to a Better Traffic Pattern" (November 8), Jerome D'Agato advocates improving Springfield's downtown traffic flow by making Main Street one-way heading south, and Clark Street one-way heading north. In my opinion, this is a blueprint for disaster.

As a traffic systems consultant, I have closely studied other cities that have traffic patterns similar to those in Springfield and that have tried this strategy. Among all the inconclusive data I reviewed, one fact is crystal clear: Alternate one-way roads work to alleviate traffic problems only if they are intersected by crossroads at least every 150 feet. This allows individual motorists on the one-way roads to exit conveniently when a change in direction is desired. Otherwise, a certain percentage of motorists remain on the one-way roads much longer than necessary or desirable.

Unfortunately, Main Street and Clark Street have numerous stretches that run longer than 150 feet without a crossroad. Indeed, one very busy stretch of both roads, from Grover Street to Maple Avenue, runs almost 800 feet without a crossroad. To impose one-way traffic on this stretch alone would create an even worse downtown traffic problem than we have now.

I urge Springfield's Traffic Planning Commission to disregard Mr. D'Agato's ill-conceived proposal and to reject any movement to make Main Street and Clark Street one-way roads.

VANESSA SIMON
Traffic Systems Consultant
State of Indiana

LETTERS TO PUBLIC OFFICIALS

In a letter to a public official, the writer is generally well advised to be very brief. Public officials are, as a rule, busy people, and most correspondence to public offices is classified and counted on a strict "for" or "against" basis, without regard to fine points.

It is perfectly adequate, and usually desirable, for the writer simply to ask for the official's support or vote without delving into the reasons. This is the best way to ensure that you communicate your principal message clearly and efficiently, without inadvertently alienating the reader with specific arguments or language.

However, there are cases when a longer letter may be warranted. If, for example, you feel especially articulate and well informed about your topic, and you have reason to believe that your reader is open-minded toward your point of view, you may well be able to help your cause by providing information, arguments, or insights that your reader may not already have.

Appearing below are examples of both types of letters to public officials: first, a simple "please support" letter; then, a more involved informational letter.

To a U.S. senator, from a private citizen urging him to support a bill (NOTE: *The writer belongs to the same political party as the senator. If she did not, she would say, "As a registered voter" instead of "As a registered Democrat."):*

Dear Senator Cartwright,

I urge you to use all your influence and your vote in support of Senate bill 290, authorizing an expansion of federal aid to the humanities. As a registered Democrat in the state of California, I feel strongly that the passage of this bill is in the best interests of the state and the nation.

Very truly yours,
ALYSSA MORROW

To the chairperson of a local school board, from a parent urging her to remove some current curriculum guidelines (NOTE: *This writer chooses to elaborate on his reasons for advocating a particular point of view. He does so because he feels they are strong and compelling reasons with which the recipient will sympathize, and because he has some relevant information to offer that the recipient may not already have.):*

Dear Chairperson Wiedenhaus,

I am very troubled by the current Gramercy school curriculum guidelines, which do not permit school libraries or classrooms to stock or recommend Mark Twain's novel *The Adventures of Huckleberry Finn*, L. Frank Baum's novel *The Wonderful Wizard of Oz*, or Judy Blume's novel *Forever*. I hope that you will do what you can to see that these ill-advised guidelines are removed.

Each of these books has been repeatedly cited by American critics and educators as a classic in children's literature. In fact, all three books appear on the recommended reading lists for elementary, middle, and high schools published by the 1993 U.S. Council on Public Education, a bipartisan White House task force. No informed and authoritative source has ever declared any of these books to be "inappropriate" for its intended audience, nor has it ever been demonstrated that reading any of these books has adversely influenced a child's moral or ethical character.

To ban these books from our school shelves without strong cause represents censorship of the most capricious and irresponsible kind. I am the parent of a daughter in Gramercy Middle School and a son in Gramercy Elementary School, who deserve to have the same constitutionally guaranteed freedom of choice that their parents had as children and that most other American children have today. It is in my children's names, too, that I ask you to remove these guidelines.

Sincerely,
JUSTIN TULL

THIRTEEN

Sales, Promotional, and Fund-raising Letters

SALES, promotional, and fund-raising letters stand apart from all other types of business letters in terms of their dramatic efforts to attract the reader's attention and persuade the reader to do something—or to feel a certain way.

- **Sales letters,** which may or may not be solicited by the reader, need to mount such a strong appeal for the reader's interest that they are almost indistinguishable from commercial advertising.
- **Promotional letters** are sent to existing customers or clients in order to keep them favorably disposed toward the writer's product or service, so it is appropriate that they are typically more restrained and businesslike than sales letters.
- **Fund-raising letters,** unlike sales or promotional letters, are designed to appeal to the reader's conscience and generosity, so the "sales pitch" aspect is necessarily more muted, but still present.

Let's look at each type of letter separately.

SALES LETTERS

Sales letters have a distinctive basic format. It's designed to move the reader through the letter in such a manner that the reader is compelled to take the action that the letter recommends. The format is as follows:

• Before even introducing the product or service, attract the reader's attention with a provocative opening statement.
• Introduce the product or service in such a manner that the reader's interest is stimulated.
• Translate the key *features* of the product or service into *benefits:* i.e., for each key feature, clarify the advantage to the purchaser, which usually results in emphasizing quality, value, and convenience.
• Close by encouraging the reader to take action.

Besides sticking to this basic format, a successful sales letter is not too short and not too long (one to one and a half pages is the optimum range); it remains positive and upbeat throughout; and it uses common, everyday language, the kind that can be understood by the largest number of people. The following examples represent the three main situations involving sales letters: selling a product, selling a service, and answering a sales inquiry.

SELLING A PRODUCT

To business managers and executives on a mailing list, regarding a news digest:

Dear Business Executive:
    Would you like to be one of the most informed and interesting people in your business community?
    Do you want to increase your ability to understand and discuss the major issues of the day by reading *less* instead of more?
    It's quick, easy, and inexpensive when you have *Business Report Weekly* delivered right to your office or home.
    Business Report Weekly offers an exclusive focus on the week's most significant business-related events, as determined for each week by a unique rotating panel of outstanding journalists. Among the panelists who frequently share their insights with readers of *Business Report Weekly* are Wayne Bolton of *New York Days;* Paula DiMartin of *World* magazine; Nathan Borowstein, the nationally syndicated columnist;

Liam O'Neill, author of the best-selling book *Time Out;* and Janet Porter of NBS-TV's *MacPherson/Lerner News Hour.*

In addition to supplying you with all the important developments relating to each week's major news stories, *Business Report Weekly* offers you all these unique and highly useful features:

- concise and intriguing *background summaries* relating to each individual story—summaries that will make it more convenient to put the latest developments into a clearer perspective;
- the *key questions* raised by each event and a wealth of intelligent responses to those questions, enabling you to evaluate different, informed points of view quickly and intelligently;
- illuminating *graphs, charts, and diagrams* that translate important facts and figures relating to each major news event into easy-to-visualize formats;
- a fascinating *comparison and contrast* discussion, clarifying the special nature of each major event in respect to similar major events in the present and the past—a service that will greatly enhance your ability to talk about the event with others.

So that you can see for yourself how informative, how exciting, and how valuable *Business Report Weekly* really is, we are offering you a special introductory subscription rate of only $49 for a full year of 52 issues! That's less than one-half of what *Business Report Weekly* would cost you on the newstand! This special rate is available for only a limited time, so please return the enclosed order card today.

Sincerely,
MICHAEL WILSON
Director of Marketing

SELLING A SERVICE

To clerical personnel who are members of a professional group, regarding adult business education classes:

Dear Career Seeker:

You can triple your chances of earning at least 50 percent more than you now earn within just two years!

If you're serious about making a good career for yourself in your chosen field of business, *Conneco College Adult Education* business classes offer you an outstanding opportunity. A recent independent study of over 1,500 clerical workers of all types proved that people who successfully complete a Conneco business course are three times as likely to be earning 50 percent more in just two years than people who do not take a Conneco business course.

Employers and students alike quickly learn to value the high-quality practical instruction and training that *Conneco College Adult Education* provides. You can choose from a wide variety of six-week or three-month courses, offered at different times during the day, week, and year to suit your personal schedule, including Accounting, Banking, Business Security, Corporate Law, Data Processing, Insurance, Investing, Management Skills, Personnel Administration, Real Estate, Sales and Marketing, and Telecommunications.

The teachers at *Conneco College Adult Education* have all had years of profitable experience in their fields, and their students reap the benefits. You'll learn from authorities how you can begin right away to get more enjoyment from your work, improve your job performance, and move up the promotion ladder. You'll get free job counseling, and you'll make valuable contacts that will help you help yourself to greater and greater business success.

And attending *Conneco College Adult Education* is easy on your wallet. You can arrange comfortable and convenient payment plans or loans, or you may qualify for one of the many scholarships provided by leading businesses in the community.

Why not check out what *Conneco College Adult Education* can offer you? It costs nothing to look, and you're sure to find something you can't afford to miss! Simply call (722) 691-2929 for free brochures and application forms, or for an appointment to talk with one of our admissions counselors.

Do it now, and in two years you, too, could be earning 50 percent more!

Sincerely,
MARTIN SANFORD
President

Responding to a Sales Inquiry

To a potential buyer who has inquired about a home security system:

Dear Mr. Pantoni,

Thank you for writing to us to express your interest in a Green Guard Home Security System. Lloyd Foley, one of our account executives, will be phoning you soon to arrange for a free, no-obligation inspection of your personal home security needs.

If Mr. Foley's professional inspection of your home indicates that you can benefit from a Green Guard Home Security System, he will explain all the options you have, demonstrate their different cost-saving benefits, and help you to arrange a convenient installation and payment schedule.

I'm sure you already realize, as other smart homeowners do, that installing the right home security system is one of the wisest investments you can make. In the greater Cincinnati area, the risk to homeowners of theft or burglary-related property damage has skyrocketed 70 percent over the past five years, and the rate of breaking and entering has more than doubled.

You and your family deserve to live in safety and security, without having to worry about intruders. We are confident that a Green Guard Home Security System can give you that comfort. We look forward to the opportunity of giving you greater peace of mind.

Yours truly,
Paul Edington
District Sales Manager

PROMOTIONAL LETTERS

A promotional letter is written to an existing client to stimulate more buying or to generate good will. Compared with a sales letter, a promotional letter is slightly less like an advertisement and slightly more like a standard business letter. The degree to which it leans one way or the other depends on the specific occasion that prompts the letter. The major occasions for writing a promotional letter to an existing customer are:

- welcoming a customer
- promoting something new or special
- introducing a company representative
- inviting a customer to a special event
- sending a customer special greetings
- offering a customer a promotional gift

The models below illustrate each of these situations.

WELCOMING A NEW CUSTOMER

*To a buyer for a recreation center who has just placed his first order from a sporting goods supplier (*NOTE: *This type of promotional letter, which refers to an actual business transaction, comes very close to being a standard business letter, except that it is noticeably more congenial and complimentary.):*

Dear Mr. Mikelovitch,

We have just shipped your order for 30 Ollirand regulation basketballs (order #3446), and they should be arriving within a few days.

I am writing to let you know how pleased we are that you have chosen Ollirand Sporting Goods as your supplier. The Meridian Recreation Center does wonderful work for the citizens of Meridian, and we are proud to be given the opportunity of serving you. We look forward to fulfilling all your sporting-goods needs promptly and efficiently.

Please contact me personally if you have any questions, comments, or requests about Ollirand products, your Ollirand orders, or how Ollirand can help you.

Thank you!

Sincerely,
DONALD PEARSE
Director of Sales

Promoting Something New or Special

To a customer, from a department store that's having a special sale (NOTE: *This type of promotional letter comes very close to being a basic sales letter, except that it's more concise and casual.*):

Dear Ms. Weiss,

Good things come to those who wait, and now the wait is over! It's time, once again, for Maxwell's annual March Right In Summer Clothing Sale! And because you are a valued Maxwell customer, we want you to know about it first.

From Friday, March 16, through Sunday, March 25, we're taking ⅓ off the price of every item of new summer clothing in Maxwell Department Store. Yes, every item! You'll save on popular brand names, like Cutty Cone sportswear, Kitty Hawk dresses, and Buzzy Bruin sandals, as well as special designer fashions, like Rinkell linen blazers, St. Protez body suits, and even Eye-Doo sunglasses. And there's much, much more!

So, march right in and enjoy Maxwell's March Right In Summer Clothing Sale! Get a head start on summer before temperatures— and prices—start rising!

Yours truly,
Mary Lou Biggs
Marketing Director

Introducing a Company Representative

To an independent bookstore owner from a director of group insurance accounts (NOTE: *This type of promotional letter is "selling" a person to the reader, a relatively formal and sophisticated task. The result is a business-like sales letter.*):

Dear Ms. Schultz,

Because Riverrun Books is a valued client of Providential Insurance Company, and has been for seven years, I wanted to let you know the good news as soon as possible.

During the upcoming week, you will receive a call from Hillary

Bascomb, an outstanding Providential account representative, who will be serving your group insurance account effective May 1. Ms. Bascomb will be replacing your current Providential representative, Marcus Pruitt, who is relocating to another area.

Ms. Bascomb has been a highly regarded Providential employee for the past five years. After graduating from Winslow University in Boston, Massachusetts, she spent two very hardworking years as a claims adjustor in our main office in Hartford, Connecticut, where she was three times named Providential Employee of the Month. She was then promoted to account administrator in the Springfield, Massachusetts, office—where she quickly earned the admiration and respect of all her clients. Now she is eager to serve as your account representative.

We want Riverrun Books to have a representative who is knowledgeable, caring, and conscientious, and Ms. Bascomb has all these qualities. We're confident that you'll like her as much as we do.

Our very best wishes for your success!

Sincerely,
PHILIP QUINN
Director, Group Accounts

INVITING A CUSTOMER TO A SPECIAL EVENT

To a manager of Esme Swank Cosmetics, from a market research firm celebrating its tenth anniversary with a party (NOTE: *If you are writing this type of promotional letter and you desire a reply, write "Please reply" or "R.s.v.p." (French for "Répondez s'il vous plaît," meaning "Please reply") in the lower left-hand corner and, directly beneath, the appropriate phone number.*):

Dear Mrs. Carswell,

Because all of us at Miles McNeal Limited have enjoyed our business relationship with you and Esme Swank Cosmetics, I would like to invite you and a guest to a special party celebrating Miles McNeal Limited's ten very successful and rewarding years as a leading market research firm.

Please join my colleagues, myself, and our honored clients—some of the best and brightest businesspeople in Minneapolis—on Friday,

September 25, 1992, from 5 p.m. to 8 p.m., at the Capri Club, 1655 DeSoto Boulevard. Come simply for the fun of it, and to give everyone at Miles McNeal a chance to demonstrate how much we value you as a client.

I hope to see you there!

> Sincerely,
> MILES MCNEAL
> President

Please reply
(415) 773-8282

SENDING A CUSTOMER SPECIAL GREETINGS

To the owner of a pet shop from a pet food supplier (NOTE: *This type of promotional letter is written solely to generate goodwill. Therefore, it should be short and sweet, and should never be used to encourage the recipient to buy anything.*):

Dear Mr. Chisholm,

I just wanted to thank you and the staff at Noah's Ark for shopping with Hilton's Pet Supply, and for helping to turn this past year into one of our best years ever. It is thoughtful and loyal customers like you who make us proud and happy to be in the pet supply business.

Have a wonderful holiday season and every success in the upcoming year!

> Very truly yours,
> MARIAN SHAUNNESSY
> Director of Marketing

OFFERING A CUSTOMER A PROMOTIONAL GIFT

Offering a client or customer a free gift is a great way of generating goodwill. Depending on the gift involved, it can also be a subtle means of interesting the recipient in making future purchases either of the gift product or service itself, or of a related product or service.

In some cases when you're writing to announce a free gift item, you may want to enclose a returnable "send" or "do not send" card, instead of the item itself. Perhaps the gift is too big or expensive simply to send out, unsolicited, to everyone; or perhaps you want to use the free-gift offer as a means of checking out which customers or clients seem to be the most responsive to sales and promotional mail.

Appearing below are examples of both types of letters: one in which the gift is enclosed and one in which a "send" or "do not send" card is enclosed instead of the gift itself.

To a doctor, from a pharmaceutical company, with the gift enclosed:

Dear Dr. Franklin,

Here is a special gift for you, at no cost or obligation, just because you are a valued customer and we want to express our appreciation.

It's an attractive and handy pad of 500 HEALTH NOTES.

Each individual sheet in the 500 HEALTH NOTES pad provides a large blank space where you, your staff member, or your patient can jot down important facts, figures, names, dates—whatever. Plus, each separate sheet offers a different, interesting, and beneficial tip for taking better care of your health, carefully compiled by our researchers from major publications of the American Medical Association.

We hope you enjoy the 500 HEALTH NOTES pad, and we look forward to serving your health care needs for many years to come!

Sincerely,
KEVIN GALLAGHER
Sales Engineer

The same letter as above, except that a "send" or "do not send" card is enclosed instead of the gift itself:

Dear Dr. Franklin,

We have a special gift for you, at no cost or obligation, just because you are a valued customer and we want to express our appreciation.

It's an attractive and handy pad of 500 HEALTH NOTES.

Each individual sheet in the 500 HEALTH NOTES pad provides a large blank space where you, your staff member, or your patient can jot down important facts, figures, names, dates—whatever. Plus, each separate sheet offers a different, interesting, and beneficial tip for taking better care of your health, carefully compiled by our researchers from major publications of the American Medical Association.

If you'd like to receive the 500 HEALTH NOTES pad as our gift, with no obligation, all you have to do is fill out and return the enclosed prestamped and preaddressed card, and we'll mail it to you right away!

We hope you'll enjoy the 500 HEALTH NOTES pad, and we look forward to serving your health care needs for many years to come.

Sincerely,
KEVIN GALLAGHER
Sales Engineer

FUND-RAISING LETTERS

In general, fund-raising letters need to be much more restrained in their tone than sales letters. After all, the writer is usually trying to engage the reader's sympathy or concern, not to stir up the reader's buying desire. Nevertheless, like a sales letter, a fund-raising letter should be strongly persuasive.

Appearing below are two examples of effective fund-raising letters. Notice how the first example is comparatively more forthright and businesslike, as befits a letter appealing to a specific individual's civic pride. By contrast, the second letter is more provocative, in the manner of a sales letter, which is appropriate given the urgent nature of the cause it promotes and the fact that it is being sent out to a mass audience. Also notice how both letters stay tightly focused on the particular organizations for which they are fund-raising, rather than flattering the reader or his or her company from time to time. This helps make the fund-raising appeal sound more earnest and sincere.

To a business executive at Intellico Corporation, from a chamber of commerce official:

Dear Mr. Kosikian,

On behalf of the city of Andover, I am respectfully asking you and Intellico Corporation to consider donating 200 choir robes to the Andover High School Chorus. This outstanding group of young men and women from the 10th, 11th, and 12th grades was recently honored with an invitation to sing at the North American Choral Festival in Vancouver, British Columbia, Canada, on January 12, 1994. We want them to look as fine as they sing!

For years, the Andover High School Chorus has made Andover proud. In 1988 it won the Northeast Choral Competition and led New York City's St. Brigid's parade. In 1989 and 1990 it helped raise over $15,000 to benefit Hurricane Harry victims. In 1992 it was selected from among 125 other choirs to sing at the Columbiania Celebration in Boston Harbor.

Now it is the Andover business community's turn to show that it is proud of the Andover High School Chorus. So far, private donations have raised $12,000 to finance the trip, and the city has pledged to match that amount. But the expenses to be covered don't include the cost of much-needed new robes.

We're counting on you to help us help the Andover High School Chorus realize its dream. Please contact me at your convenience, and let me know whether you will support this worthy effort.

Thank you.

> Sincerely,
> RUTH DIMMANANCI
> Vice President, Chamber of Commerce

To subscribers to a conservation magazine, from a conservation group:

Dear Wilderness Lover,

We're fighting to save America the Beautiful!

Every day, in every year, in every state of America, a battle rages between the forces of self-interest and the forces of nature, and the forces of nature are slowly but surely losing. The amount of wilderness converted to industrial or agricultural use keeps going up, and the number of animals, plants, trees, and unpolluted waterways keeps going down.

Won't you help us fight back, so that America can remain beautiful?

The Sea-to-Sea Conservation Society conducts environmental

studies all across America that help prevent industry and agriculture from destroying natural habitats. The Sea-to-Sea Conservation Society also lobbies federal and state government agencies, designs educational programs for schools, and sponsors resource-recovery efforts through its innovative "By Land or By Sea" program.

Why not join the fight!

We desperately need any size donation you can make—$5, $10, $20, $100—so that we can continue and, ultimately, win the fight to save America the Beautiful. Won't you help? Please send a check or money order (no cash) in the enclosed prestamped, preaddressed envelope.

Thank you for listening to our battle cry!

                   Sincerely,

                   STEVE REILLY

                   President, Sea-to-Sea Conservation Society

FOURTEEN

Memorandums

A MEMORANDUM (commonly referred to as a "memo") is a type of interoffice or intercolleague communication that is brisker and more efficient than the standard business letter. Its uniquely streamlined format sets the style. Instead of the usual introductory parts of the letter—heading, dateline, inside address, and greeting, a memo begins with four simple entries: To:, From:, Date:, Re: (or Subject:). (See the Appendix for letter and memo formats.)

The text of a memo is typically stripped of all frills and organized for maximum clarity and convenience, frequently employing subtitles, bulleted lists, or other streamlining devices to make key points stand out. Often, at the same time that the memo is sent to the addressee(s), copies are sent to all other individuals concerned with the issue being discussed. If this is being done, it is indicated at the top or the bottom of the memo with the designation "copies:" or "cc:" (for "carbon copy," a once common form of duplication), followed by the names of all people receiving copies (see Appendix).

Common purposes for which a memo is used include the following:

- announcing new developments
- requesting information or action
- clarifying or codifying a policy or recent discussion

- issuing assignments
- reporting progress

Here are some examples of these kinds of memos:

To East-West Products personnel, from the president, announcing a record sales volume (NOTE: *The style of this memo is somewhat more effusive than the standard memo style because the writer wants to take advantage of an appropriate opportunity to boost company morale.*):

I am pleased to report that East-West Products sold a record $995,000 worth of Paisley Pagodas during the last quarter (April 1 through June 30). You are all to be commended for your help in making this our most successful season ever.

As you know, our goal for this quarter is $110,000. With your good work, I am confident we can reach it!

To Continental Footwear's director of research and development, from a department manager, applying for a paid trip:

I would like to request that Continental send me as its representative to the 23rd Annual Convention of Camping and Sporting Goods, December 3 through 7, 1994, in Denver, Colorado.

For the past two months, I have been the supervisor of a team working to develop a line of inexpensive and comfortable hiking and climbing shoes for the "easy use" market. I am confident that this convention will give me unique opportunities to talk with others in the field about such products, as well as to investigate more closely what the competition has to offer.

Attached is a brochure describing the conference and listing fees and price ranges in local accommodations. I would appreciate a quick response, so that I can plan my November and December work schedules well in advance.

Please call me if any further information would be helpful.

To Larko sales managers, from Larko's vice president of sales, announcing a change in policy:

Effective immediately, all orders of 24 or more Larko products with a suggested retail price of $10 or less per unit are to be sold at a discount as follows:

- 10 percent price discount for orders of 24 through 48 units
- 15 percent price discount for orders exceeding 48 units

In addition to encouraging more total orders for these products, this policy is designed to convert traditional low-volume, high-frequency orderers into high-volume, low-frequency orderers, thus saving us shipping, handling, and administrative costs.

Specifically, this policy applies to the following Larko products currently in production:

- Larko Bath Beads: $9.90 per unit
- Larko Bath Sponges: $9.10/$7.50/$6.00 per unit
- Larko Shower Gel: $5.60 per unit
- Larko Bubble Bath: $3.50 per unit
- Larko Soap (bath size): $2.35 per unit
- Larko Soap (regular): $1.75 per unit

Any Larko product costing less than $10.00 per unit that is added to the line in the future will also be eligible for these discounts.

Please see that all customers, distributors, and Larko personnel are made aware of this policy, and direct any questions or responses to my office.

To Magnus departmental supervisors, from the Magnus personnel director, making a request for information:

All Magnus employees need a common source of reference for better understanding their own and their coworkers' job responsibilities and reporting functions. To help our department prepare an effect organizational chart and job description manual, please give one of the attached job description forms to each of the employees in your department and ask him or her to complete it.

All completed forms should be reviewed by you and returned to me no later than Monday, September 16.

To all Whitman and Company personnel, from the director of security, clarifying a policy:

Many Whitman and Company personnel have expressed confusion or lack of information regarding the current policy of signing in and signing out of the building. I am writing to clarify this policy and appeal for your help in making it work.

Per guidelines effective December 15, 1994, all guests entering the building, at any time, whether or not they are accompanied by an employee, are required to do the following:

1. Sign the register at the reception desk before proceeding further into the building.
2. When signing the register, write their names, the office (name and number) to which they are going, and the time.
3. Pick up a "Guest Tag" from the receptionist and wear it in an easily visible spot on their persons at all times during their stay.
4. Just before leaving the building, stop at the reception desk and sign out, indicating their sign-out time in the space next to their previously registered sign-in time.

All <u>employees</u> are expected to follow the same process (except for #3, wearing the "Guest Tag") when entering or leaving the building before 9 a.m. or after 6 p.m. If an employee enters the building before 9 a.m. and leaves sometime between 9 a.m. and 6 p.m., he or she does need to sign in, but does not need to sign out. If an employee enters the building sometime between 9 a.m. and 6 p.m. and leaves after 6 p.m., he or she does not need to sign in, but does need to sign out.

Compliance with this policy helps us to identify and manage traffic, maintenance, and security needs for the entire building and each office inside it. Your kind cooperation would be greatly appreciated.

To PBC Inc.'s shipping and receiving manager, from the company's vice president, issuing an assignment:

Please locate several suitable, new, long-term storage facility sites for backup inventory as soon as possible. I would like to have all backup inventory moved from its present on-site warehouse to a nearby outside location by November 1 at the latest. This move is intended to clear the on-site warehouse for predelivery storage.

Look for sites that offer the same amount of space we currently use, but are capable of expansion, if necessary, to meet future needs. The maximum price we're willing to pay is $15 per square foot.

Report progress to me by June 7 or as soon as you've located three potential sites, whichever comes first.

To Halliwell Brothers' design department manager, from the director of sales training, inquiring about an overdue order (NOTE: *The writer of this memo is very concerned about the delay and wants interested parties to be aware of what is happening. Therefore, she is using this memo to record the history of the situation for the benefit of the interested parties, who are all receiving copies.*):

When will we receive the 1,000 copies of the new brochure, "Meeting Needs," that we requested on March 3 (order #CG-233-94)? I need a specific, guaranteed delivery date as soon as possible, so that subsidiaries can schedule long-overdue training sessions.

At the time I placed the order, I said that our department needed these brochures as soon as possible in order to respond to rapidly increasing demand from our subsidiaries. I was told the brochures would arrive by March 24. When they did not, I called you directly and was told that all appropriate paper was temporarily out of stock and wouldn't be available until June 1. I was then given a new delivery date for the brochures of "around June 15." The brochures have still not arrived.

I would appreciate your giving this matter prompt, personal attention.

To Americo's vice president of corporate affairs, from the public relations director, reporting on an assignment:

Here is a report on our February 1 through March 1 activities to promote Americo's "Arbor Day Extravaganza":

Media Coverage

- Distributed press kits to all local radio, television, and newspaper contacts, and followed up with telephone inquiries.
- Held two-hour press conference on February 6 to announce initial plans for project.

<u>Planning and Preparation</u>

- Submitted final schedule and budget for festival activities.
- Established four-member departmental committee for full-time work on festival.
- Recruited student and faculty representatives from each local school to facilitate "What's in a Tree?" program.

<u>Special Projects</u>

- Signed Raven Le Noire and Paul Whiteside to lead "Parade of Trees."
- Donated 20 cherry trees to line Logan Pond.

To the director of Providential group insurance accounts, from a Providential group insurance administrator, reporting on a problem situation:

Per your request, I have investigated the practice among many Providential sales representatives of submitting one combined premium for all of a client's Providential accounts (group health, life, auto, and property), rather than separate premiums for each account. After consulting with numerous sales representatives who do and do not follow this practice, as well as with sales managers, accountants, and administrators, I am submitting this report.

<u>The problem</u>

Many sales representatives say that their clients find it easier to make one combined payment to Providential rather than several smaller, account-by-account payments. The reps also say that it's easier for them to track and collect one payment than several.

However, the one-payment strategy creates problems for home office accountants and administrators. Often, the entire premium is credited to only one account, resulting in a carry-over credit, instead of being distributed appropriately among all relevant accounts. This sometimes happens even when the premium is accompanied by a cover letter explaining how it is to be divided, or when the different account numbers are marked on the premium check itself.

<u>Key issues</u>

- The sales representatives currently facilitating the one-payment policy are reluctant to withdraw this option from their clients. The reps see it as a good marketing tool, offering clients convenience and helping to minimize client complaints about individual account premiums. There's much concern that they will lose accounts and "lose face" if they have to retract this courtesy.

- The accounting department cannot guarantee a reduction of problems associated with the one-payment practice unless it institutes more attentive personal handling of every premium check. This cannot be done in a cost-effective manner.

- Upon receiving a one-payment check, the accounting department cannot assign dollar amounts to different accounts, since the current procedure calls for matching the check number with the account number. Instead, the accounting department has to deposit the check in its own account and then write separate checks of its own to cover the different accounts. This results in more time and cost for the department, and it delays payment.

- Administrators ultimately are left with the task of straightening out problems associated with the single-payment policy. It is not routine practice to check for a misassigned payment in the case of a computer-reported credit or debit, nor would it be cost-efficient to make it a routine practice. As a result, a single-payment problem doesn't manifest itself until a related problem arises between the administrator and the client or the administrator and the sales representative.

Recommended actions

- Discontinue the present informal, one-payment practice. Insist upon compliance with the standard policy of submitting a separate payment for each account.

  At present, clients allowed to make one big payment are highly susceptible to being told by Providential administrators that they are delinquent in certain accounts when, in fact, they have paid their full premium. The indignation clients would feel in this situation is a much more serious danger to Providential than the aggravation they might feel at having to write several smaller checks instead of one big check.

- Consider creating a new "Super-account" program, in which clients with multiple accounts could submit a single payment covering all their accounts. This program would necessitate creating new premium forms as well as new premium-allotment procedures affecting the sales, accounting, and administration departments.

Please let me know if you need any additional information or if I can be of further service.

FIFTEEN

Resumés and Application Letters

JOB APPLICANTS are expected to submit a formal resumé out-lining their job-related qualifications to every prospective employer. In some situations, no other document is required: for example, when the applicant is working through a company's personnel department to consider any appropriate job in that company, or when the employment interview is so informal or so quickly scheduled that the applicant simply hands the resumé to the interviewer during their conversation. In most situations, however, a resumé is sent by a job applicant to a prospective employer as a means of soliciting an interview, in which case the resumé needs to be introduced by an application letter. Let's look at resumés first and then consider application letters.

BASIC FORMATS FOR RESUMÉS

A resumé is a concise business-style report that displays your job qualifications to a prospective employer. Like your personal appearance in a face-to-face interview, the physical appearance, or format, of your resumé is very important in its own right, testifying to your initiative, ability to communicate, and overall professionalism. Even more important to your job-hunting success, however, is the content of your resumé: the listing of those specific skills, employment experiences, professional achievements, and educational and training accomplishments that make you a likely candidate for the kind of job you are seeking.

In a resumé, format and content are inseparably linked. There are three basic resumé formats (described below), which you can customize to suit your particular needs: *employer-based, role-based,* and *skill-based.* The challenge for you as a resumé writer is to choose the one basic format that will best highlight your particular assortment of qualifications. Before you can do this, you must consider two main issues:

1. What type of job hunter are you: inexperienced, experienced, or job changer?

- Is this your first job? Or is it only your second job in the same field? If so, you are relatively *inexperienced* in terms of job hunting.
- Is this your third, fourth, or fifth job in the same field? If so, you are relatively *experienced* in this sort of job hunt.
- Is this job significantly different from the job(s) you've had before? Does it represent a career shift? Or is it the latest job in a string of different types of jobs? If so, you are a *job changer.*

2. What is the major area of strength among your qualifications: employers, roles, or skills?

- An *employer-based* resumé may be the most appropriate format choice in the following circumstances:

  ——You are an *experienced* job seeker who has spent many years in the same field, working for several prestigious employers.
  ——You are relatively *inexperienced* in the full-time job market, but you've had numerous part-time or volunteer jobs with impressive organizations.

- A *role-based* resumé may be the most appropriate format choice in the following circumstances:

  ——You are an *experienced* job seeker who has moved steadily up the ranks within a given field, possibly involving one or more changes of employer.
  ——You have performed several important functions under one

job title, including functions that may not automatically be associated with that particular title.

——The list of roles you have fulfilled is much more impressive than the list of places where you have worked.

- A *skill-based* resumé may be the most appropriate format choice in the following circumstances:

  ——You are relatively *inexperienced* in terms of full-time work, but you have accumulated plenty of work-related capabilities through part-time jobs, voluntary service, or trainee experience.

  ——You have acquired a great number of skills after relatively few years of full-time employment.

  ——You are a *job changer* and want to emphasize your overall skills as opposed to your specific employment history.

  ——You don't want to draw attention to gaps, reversals, or complications in your employment history.

The three major resumé formats are presented below, with sample resumés in each format to reflect a variety of different job-hunt situations. First, however, here are guidelines that apply to writing any resumé, regardless of its format.

General Guidelines

- Try to limit the length of your resumé to a single page for the convenience of the reader. This may not be possible if you have an extensive work history (e.g., over fifteen years). In this case, make every effort to be as concise as you reasonably can. If you have numerous publications, consultations, or honors to your credit, consider listing them separately on another, supplemental page.
- Bear in mind that some information that you *could* provide in your resumé may, in fact, be unnecessary or even unhelpful. For example, you may not want to list jobs that you held over ten years ago if they are not related to the job you are presently seeking, or you may not want to call attention to skills that you

have or positions you've held if you really do not want to use those skills or hold those positions again.

- Offer your name, address, and phone number at the very top of the resumé, followed by a statement of the job title you are seeking (commonly known as the "Job Objective"). The rest of the page can be arranged according to the general format you've chosen, the nature of the qualifications you are expressing, and your own stylistic preferences (see the model resumés below for ideas).

- Allow ample margins at the top, bottom, and sides of the page, and use appropriate blocking and spacing within the text. This ensures that your resumé as a whole has sufficient "white space" and is therefore easier and more pleasant to read.

- Confine yourself to outlining your *professional* skills, roles, employment history, and achievements as efficiently as possible. Avoid mentioning *personal* matters like age, sex, height, weight, health condition, marital status, and hobbies, and avoid using adjectives that are pointedly self-praising (e.g., "loyal," "outstanding," "well-respected").

- Do not list references or mention past and current bosses by proper name. This type of information is best communicated during or after the interview itself, not only so that you can give each potential employer the names that best suit the situation at hand, but also so that you can help protect your references and present or past bosses from receiving too many unexpected calls. If appropriate and desired, you can state at the bottom of your resumé, "References available on request."

EMPLOYER-BASED RESUMÉS

The most traditional of the three basic resumé formats, the employer-based resumé lists the applicant's work history according to the organizations where he or she has worked, going in chronological order from the present back through the past (ten years is sufficient). If specific job titles are used, only one title is given for each organizational entry: the highest title achieved while working at that organization. Offered below are examples of this type of resumé for each of the three main types of job seekers: inexperienced, experienced, and job changer.

The following employer-based resumé is written by a homemaker who is inexperienced in terms of full-time employment but who has noteworthy experience in terms of volunteer work for highly regarded organizations:

MARILYN FRENAULT

1832 Academy Street   Columbus, OH 43220
(614) 771-9026

Goal: administrative position in a social service organization

Work Experience

American Red Cross, Columbus, OH   1989–present

- organized and conducted city-wide "Bloodmobile" drives for four years
- trained volunteers in crisis-related functions
- wrote proposals and business reports

Haven Home, St. Ann's Cathedral, Columbus, OH   1991–present

- assisted in founding 30-bed shelter for the homeless
- interviewed, hired, trained, and supervised volunteer staff members and two paid staff positions
- acted as admissions officer and referral agent

State of Ohio, Welfare Department   1989–1991

- lectured and led workshops throughout the central Ohio area on avoiding or overcoming substance abuse, as part of the state's "Down on Drugs" program
- conducted and compiled research on substance abuse

In-Crisis Service, Moriah Hospital, Dayton, OH   1986–1988

- counseled people in crisis over the telephone and face to face, including substance abusers, would-be suicides, and people with serious illnesses
- helped design and conduct fund-raising projects

Education

B.A., psychology
Ohio State University, Columbus, OH   1984

Graduate studies (18 hours), social work
Ohio State University, Columbus, OH   1984–1986

References available on request.

_____

Written by a person who is experienced in his field, the following employer-based resumé also draws special attention to language skills, since they may well be important in the job for which he's applying:

JOHN DELANEY   1556 East 79th Street, #16D
                                      New York, NY 10021
                                      (212) 456-3777

Position desired: managing editor of a magazine

1986–present   *McCoy's Journal* New York, NY   Editor

- plan, solicit, evaluate, and edit news, information, and feature articles
- hire, train, and supervise assistant editors and reporters
- work closely with photographers, artists, and designers on visuals
- prepare and administer budgets
- coordinate monthly staff meetings

1984–1986   *Sports Review* New York, NY   Associate Editor

  • received, selected, edited, and rewrote manuscripts
  • wrote copy for news and feature articles
  • monitored galley production
  • represented magazine at conferences

1981–1984   *Daily Newsworld* New York, NY   Reporter

  • researched and wrote local news, feature, and sports stories
  • wrote weekly column "In Training" (1983-1984)
  • won 1984 Gotham Press Award for Excellence in Feature Writing

Education:

1980   B.A. in Journalism, Northwestern University, Evanston, IL
1980–1981   Graduate studies in journalism
             (15 hours),
             Columbia University, New York, NY

Foreign Languages:

             Fluent in Spanish and German; reading knowledge of French

Writing samples available on request.

The employer-based resumé below was written by a job changer, *whose "inside" familiarity with a variety of different companies helps qualify him for the job he's seeking:*

Eric Kingman
190 Maple Avenue
Dallas, TX 75231
(214) 222-5434

Objective: sales account manager for a service organization

Employment History:

Providence Insurance Company Dallas, TX

1990–present

Claims Manager for group insurance accounts: develop and maintain accounts: issue final claims decisions; supervise staff of 22 claims and customer service representatives; report directly to Corporate Affairs Division.

Mutual of Fort Worth Fort Worth, TX   1987–1990

Senior Claims Representative for individual and group policies: worked closely with account managers to sell and develop accounts; investigated claims and advised on payments.

Bank of the United States New York, NY   1985–1987

Customer Service Trainer for regional bank personnel in New England and South Central United States: designed and conducted workshops; wrote training materials; researched and evaluated sales and marketing strategies.

Education:

B.S., Marketing, Lee University, Charlottesville, VA   1985
Allied Training Institute, Bank of the United States,
New York, NY   1985–1986

Awards:

Lowman Award for Business Achievement, Dallas Chamber of
Commerce, Dallas, TX   1992

Outstanding Trainer, National Association of
Trainers, Denver, CO   1987

ROLE-BASED RESUMÉS

In a role-based resumé the applicant expresses his or her work history by emphasizing the various job functions he or she has fulfilled. This format shows that the applicant has "worn many hats." It's especially appropriate for applicants who have held a variety of positions within the same field, and whose job objective could involve any one of a number of possible titles. Offered below are examples of this type of resumé for each of the three main types of job seekers: inexperienced, experienced, and job changer.

The following resumé, written by an inexperienced *college graduate, makes it clear that the applicant has, in fact, assumed various impressive job roles, despite the fact that he has never been a full-time employee (an accompanying application letter appears on pages 208–209):*

David Morris O'Reilly
16643 Ocean Avenue
Brooklyn, NY 14221
(718) 553-6938

Career Goal: a position in biochemical research

EXPERIENCE

Laboratory Technician   1992–1994
- conducted study of sea mussel habitat preservation in Long Island Sound, funded by the Atlantic Institute and the New York State Government
- monitored pollution levels in public waterlands in Nassau County, NY, under the supervision of the NY State Department of the Interior

Research Assistant   1989–1992
- participated in Dr. Sandra Endicott's study of the effects of acid rain on marine microorganisms
- regularly ran tests to measure oxygen, hydrogen, chlorophyll, and saline levels in marine wetlands

- maintained all public-access laboratory records for Long Island State University

Science Writer   1990–1994
- wrote monthly column on oceanography, "At Sea," for Long Island State University's *Journal*
- published science-related articles in national periodicals, including *Science Life*, *Sea to Sea*, and *Natural History*

EDUCATION

M.A., Ecology, Long Island State University,
Seaview, NY   1994
B.S., Biology, Long Island State University,
Seaview, NY   1992

AWARDS

Tischler Prize for Excellence in Science   1994
American Science Foundation Scholarship   1988–1992

References and writing samples available upon request.

The role-based resumé below was written by an experienced *job applicant who wants prospective employers to notice that she has risen steadily through the ranks of her career in a relatively short period of time (an accompanying application letter appears on page 209):*

MARY ALICE WHITNEY
2525 El Tommorando Road
Oakland, CA 94611
(510) 226-0897

Job Target

Manager of Purchasing Department
in a retail clothing store with national outlets

Work History

<u>Buyer in Women's Clothing</u>
Jericho's, San Francisco, CA   1991 to present
• buy fashions for 16 stores in three states
• supervise staff of 20 at main store and outlets
• prepare sales reports and marketing projections
• coordinate catalog sales

<u>Associate Buyer in Women's Clothing</u>
Main Mart, San Francisco, CA   1989–1991
• bought fashions for main store and three outlets
• supervised staff of 10 at main store
• designed and conducted seasonal customer surveys

<u>Assistant Buyer</u>
The Gold Store, Anaheim, CA   1988–1990
• bought fashions for "Big and Beautiful" boutique
• supervised five salesclerks
• won "Seller of the Month" award seven times

<u>Customer Service Representative</u>
Kelly Department Store, Los Angeles, CA   1986–1988
• sold women's fashions in all lines
• participated in buying decisions
• wrote sales reports

Education

Orange County Community College   1985–1987
Anaheim High School (graduate)   1984

References available on request.

This role-based resumé is written by a job changer *who has always been a dietician in the past, but who now seeks a management position within a health-related service organization.* (NOTE: *Each time this resumé is submitted, the "Goal" line is customized, using a word processor, to state the particular name of the organization.*)

Rosa Cremonelli
1392 Briarwood Avenue
Eau Claire, WI 54701
(715) 443-7172

<u>Goal:</u> management position with the American Diabetes Foundation

<u>Positions Held</u>

<u>Nutritionist</u>
• consulted with individuals and groups regarding diets for proper health management
• evaluated nutritional aspects of food service programs in business cafeterias and schools
• wrote a series of widely used pamphlets: *Coping with Special Dietary Needs*

<u>Administrator</u>
• planned and supervised food service programs in hospitals and schools
• hired, trained, and supervised food service personnel
• prepared food service budgets up to $750,000 annually
• researched and wrote food service business reports

<u>Instructor</u>
• designed and taught instructional programs on Therapeutic Nutrition, Nutrition and Food Service, and Diet and Eating Disorders
• lectured on nutrition and diet for adult education, business, and civic groups
• conducted workshops on nutrition for hospital personnel

<u>Employment</u>
1987–present	Chief Dietician, Riverside Hospital, Eau Claire, WI
1983–1987	Instructor, Department of Diet and Nutrition, Acme University, Minneapolis, MN
1984–1988	Dietician, Halcyon Community College, Halcyon, MN

1978–1984   Director of Food Service, Wyntton, Inc., Minneapolis, MN

Education
M.S., Nutrition, Wisconsin University, Milton, WI, 1977
B.S., Chemistry, Wisconsin State University, Paradise, WI, 1974

Memberships
ADA Registry
Wisconsin Dietetic Association
U.S. Department of Agriculture's Food Group Panel (1991-1992)

SKILL-BASED RESUMÉS

A skill-based resumé focuses on the major work-related skills the writer possesses, isolating each particular skill and analyzing the different ways in which the writer used that skill successfully in a working context. Secondary attention is given to the writer's actual employment history. Offered below are examples of this type of resumé for each of the three main types of job seekers: inexperienced, experienced, and job changer.

Written by a just-graduated college student who is relatively inexperienced, this skill-based resumé emphasizes capabilities and accomplishments that pertain to the job being sought. At the same time it effectively downplays the writer's lack of full-time work experience.

Marguerite DiSantis

1772 Guilford Avenue   St. Louis, MO 63116
(314) 555-2277

OBJECTIVE: artist for an advertising agency

SKILLS

Illustration: numerous line drawings for commercial periodicals, slides, and promotional materials

Photography: three years of photojournalism for university and local newspapers

| *Design:* | experienced in every aspect of production from layout to finish, pasteups, and reproduction |

EXPERIENCE

Production Assistant, *One World* magazine, Chicago, IL, summers 1991–1994

Photographer, *Tri-Village Bulletin*, Wiltondale, MO, 1991–1994

Photographer, *USL News*, University of St. Louis, St. Louis, MO, 1991–1994

Chief Designer, *Credo* yearbook, University of St. Louis, St. Louis, MO, 1993–1994

EDUCATION

B.A. in Commercial Art, University of St. Louis, St. Louis, MO, 1994

Chicago Art Academy Institute, Chicago, IL, 1993

References and work samples available on request.

———

The following skill-based resumé reflects a person who is relatively experienced *in the field of his job objective and who has acquired more professional capabilities than his current and previous job titles indicate:*

CLIFFORD WELLES
1194 St. Augustine Boulevard
Atlanta, GA 30354
(404) 986-4888

Position desired: director of public relations

Public relations skills

- exclusive, concurrent management of all public relations activities for seven corporate clients
- preparation and management of $2 million annual budget
- supervision of 15-member staff
- publicity development for products and services
- purchase of advertising time in all broadcast and cable media

- purchase of advertising space in national, regional, and local periodicals
- composition, editing, and release of news items
- development and leadership of company meetings and trade shows
- scheduling and supervision of news conferences

Employment history

1990 to present	Kincaid & Lowther, Inc., Atlanta, GA
	Senior Account Executive
1985–1990	Capitol Public Relations, Inc., Washington, DC
	Public Relations Manager
1981–1985	Allied Advertising Corporation Richmond, VA
	Assistant Manager, Public Relations

Education

| 1981 | M.B.A., Drake University, Raleigh, NC |
| 1978 | B.A. in Business, Colerain College, Atlanta, GA |

The following skill-based resumé highlights the impressive and relevant skills accumulated by a person who is a job changer and, what's more, has a history of changing jobs. (NOTE: The resumé itself mentions several book and video titles, to give an idea of the types of projects involved. A separate page offers a complete list of books and videos, with full publication or production data for each entry. An accompanying application letter appears on page 210.)

Diane Harrington Banks
11 Fairmount Terrace, #6G
Phoenix, AZ 85028
(602) 791-3434

Objective: Instructor, Communication Arts

Writing and Editing

- wrote nonfiction books for trade market, including *Your Child in School, Get Time on Your Side,* and *Coping with Serious Illness*
- evaluated, revised, and edited manuscripts for publication
- researched, wrote, and edited scripts for video productions
- wrote and edited articles for national magazines

Video Production

- designed instructional and informational programming for business and institutional markets, including *Learning to Listen* and *Writing for Results*
- hired and supervised directors, cast, crew, writers, and consultants
- developed production budgets, formats, and schedules
- oversaw filming and editing of videotape masters

Library Science

- designed and conducted public education programs on library-related topics for schools and institutions
- researched client and staff reference queries
- administered reserve and reference system for main library and nine branches

Work History

1990–present	producer, Trans-America Video, Inc., Phoenix, AZ
1988–1990	freelance writer
1986–1988	editor, Iron Mountain Press, Denver, CO
1985–1988	assistant librarian, Bannerton Public Library System, Bannerton, CO

Educational Background

B.A., Language and Literature, Zenith University, Boston, MA, 1983

M.A., Communications, Cornwall University, Delphi, NY, 1985

APPLICATION LETTERS

An application letter accompanies and introduces a resumé when the resumé is being mailed to a prospective employer. An application letter should always be addressed to a specific individual. If in doubt, call the organization to which you're applying and ask for the most appropriate name to use. It's generally best to apply to the highest-ranking person involved.

The main purpose of an application letter is to interest the recipient in granting you a personal interview. In the opening paragraph of the letter, you should clarify which specific job you want and how you learned about the job vacancy (or, if no particular job vacancy is involved, why you are writing to this person at this time about this job). The letter should go on to state, in summary fashion, why you want the job and why you qualify for it. It should end by requesting an interview, indicating your availability (ideally, at any time), and providing information on how to contact you (ideally, this will be as simple and easy as phoning one number at any time).

Here are other guidelines for composing an effective application letter:

• Be concise. Generally speaking, an application letter shouldn't be longer than one page.

• Avoid bragging or boasting. Call attention to your most impressive achievements relating to the job you are seeking, and let these achievements speak for themselves.

- Do not state the specific salary range or job circumstances you expect. It is better to communicate this type of information in a face-to-face interview, where there's a forum for negotiation.
- Be conservative and professional in your approach. Attempts to attract attention by being humorous, folksy, intellectual, or unorthodox can easily offend potential employers, especially if they are seeking someone who conforms to a particular company image or who can be an effective team player.
- Remain positive throughout your letter. Try not to say negative things about present or past employment experiences, or about your own qualifications compared with the potential demands of the position for which you're applying.

Appearing below are different examples of well-written acceptance letters covering a variety of different job-seeking situations. Notice how each writer not only summarizes his or her personal work experience relating to the position being sought, but also acknowledges the needs and interests of the potential employer.

___

An inexperienced *college graduate, applying for a position in biochemical research (accompanying resumé appears on pages 199–200):*

Dear Dr. Rickles,
Dr. Sandra Endicott, professor of biology at Long Island State University, told me that you are seeking a biochemical researcher at Kerrigan Industries. I am very interested in Kerrigan Industries and would like to be considered for the position. Enclosed is my resumé.
According to Dr. Endicott, you are looking for a scientist to help design and conduct studies of marine flora and fauna. This field of biochemistry has been my specialty throughout my undergraduate and graduate studies at Long Island State University. I enjoy team research as well as independent fieldwork, and I'm eager to assist you in whatever capacity best serves your interests.
In 1994 my research on sea mussel habitats in Long Island Sound earned me the Tischler Prize for Excellence in Science. It also made me appreciate the importance of the type of high-quality research that Kerrigan has performed in this area. I would welcome the opportunity to share my skills and expand my knowledge by working with you and your colleagues.

Please let me know when it would be convenient for us to meet, and I will make myself available. You can reach me at (718) 553-6938.

Thank you for your consideration.

Sincerely,
(signature)
DAVID O'REILLY

enclosure

An experienced *job seeker, applying for a job as manager of a purchasing department (accompanying resumé appears on pages 200–201):*

Dear Ms. Heilford,

I was happy to read in *Women's Fashion Monthly* that Tracy's Department Stores has an opening for a purchasing department manager. I have always admired your organization, and I'm sending you my resumé in the hope that you will consider me for this position.

In your notice you said that you wanted a manager with a wide range of experience who has innovative ideas and who can motivate sales personnel. I'm confident that I can give you the expertise and commitment you seek. Over the past eight years, I have bought all lines of women's fashions, including sportswear, casual fashions, and formal fashions. I have progressed rapidly from being a customer service representative in a single-store outlet to being the buyer for 16 Jericho's stores, where I design sales strategies and manage 20 very skilled and enthusiastic staff members.

I would like to meet with you, at your convenience, to discuss your specific needs. Please leave a message at any time with my answering service, (510) 226-0897, and I will respond promptly. I look forward to hearing from you.

Yours truly,
(signature)
MARY ALICE WHITNEY

enclosure

A job changer, *applying for a job as a college or university instructor in communication arts, without knowing whether or not there is a specific job opening (the accompanying resumé appears on pages 206–207):*

Dear Dr. McMartin,

I am sending you my resumé in hopes that you will consider employing me as an instructor of communication arts at Fairview University. I have long wanted to teach communication arts to college students, and Fairview University attracts the kind of creative, self-motivated, and job-oriented people that I believe I can help the most.

As my enclosed resumé makes clear, I would be coming to such a position with a fresh point of view, having accumulated a wide range of practical skills and experience in writing and editing manuscripts, producing instructional video courses, and coordinating library-related education programs with schools. In all of these endeavors, I've acted successfully to inform, lead, and evaluate the performances of others. At Fairview I would be open to fulfilling a variety of functions involving teaching, interdepartmental coordination, and community service, according to your particular needs and interests.

If my qualifications interest you, please call me anytime at (602) 791-3434 to set up an interview. The best time for me to travel to Fairview would be on a Thursday, Friday, or Monday.

Thank you.

Sincerely,
(signature)
DIANE HARRINGTON BANKS

enclosure

SIXTEEN

Letters of Acceptance, Rejection, and Resignation

LETTERS OF ACCEPTANCE

A person who is expressing acceptance to someone generally has two purposes to accomplish:

1. announcing the acceptance itself, which is a positive response to a submission or application made by the recipient; and
2. instructing the recipient about the consequences of this acceptance, i.e., the benefits and responsibilities that are inherent and the next "action steps" to be taken.

How the acceptor chooses to fulfill these two purposes depends on the particular situation at hand, but the announcement itself is almost always made official by a letter of acceptance.

Some writers link both purposes in their letters of acceptance by being consistently motivational. Their letters focus quickly on the excitement of their news and proceed to frame each subsequent benefit, responsibility, or action step in positive, enthusiastic terms. Other writers prefer to write an acceptance letter that concentrates mainly on the happiness of the announcement itself. They fulfill the instructional purpose by enclosing separate enclosures (e.g., a contract or a list of action steps) or by waiting for a subsequent meeting or telephone conversation.

The approach you should take in expressing your acceptance

depends on the situation at hand. If you prefer to communicate instructions in person, or if you have a large number of instructions to communicate, then you may want to minimize the instructional function of your acceptance letter. In contrast, if you want to make sure that the accepted person recognizes and appreciates certain key instructions, or if you have relatively few instructions to issue, then you may want to use the acceptance letter to transmit instructions. The latter approach is often taken when copies of the letter of acceptance are being sent to other people who have a vested interest in knowing what is expected of the recipient.

No matter what type of acceptance letter you are writing, here are some general guidelines to follow:

- The body of an acceptance letter should be relatively formal in tone, even when the personal relationship between the writer and the recipient is informal. Think of an acceptance letter as an official document, one that is likely to be kept in a file and read by others. Keep in mind that some acceptance letters (such as those accepting an application for employment) have a quasi-legal status. Therefore, you don't want to say anything frivolous or open to the wrong interpretation.
- Within the first paragraph of the letter, express the acceptance and be specific regarding any new title that comes with the acceptance. Also, be sure that the body of the letter specifies all of the major conditions of the acceptance that are likely to determine the recipient's response (e.g., salary for a position, deadline for an assignment, tasks that must be completed before the acceptance takes effect).
- Avoid detailed reference to the process you went through to accept the applicant. It is no longer relevant, and your focus should be on the future.

Here are some examples of different types of acceptance letters applying to various common situations:

To an applicant for the position of associate director of marketing at P.J. Guilford, Inc., from the vice president of marketing (NOTE: *In this "acceptance-of-an-applicant" situation, the writer frames the acceptance as an "offer." He also greets the recipient informally, by first name, which is appropriate to the organization's style and to the friendliness of his previous encounters with the recipient. For two possible "yes" responses to the letter, see the two letters immediately following it.):*

Dear Ruth,

It gives me great pleasure to offer you the position of associate director of marketing at P.J. Guilford, Inc. Our meetings with you over the past months have convinced us that your administrative talents, knowledge of the field, and personal energy are exactly what we want for this important function. Our president, P.J. Guilford, agrees and is eager to welcome you into our organization.

I am prepared to offer you an initial annual salary of $55,000 with a substantial package of benefits and incentive options, as described in the enclosed Confidential Personnel Memorandum. You are already familiar with the key job responsibilities associated with this position, but for convenient reference, I will briefly outline them here as they appear in our *Organizational Manual:*

- To cooperate with the director of marketing in planning, development, and administrating sales and marketing programs and campaigns.
- To cooperate with the director of marketing in keeping company management informed in a timely and efficient manner about sales and marketing developments and results.
- To recruit, train, supervise, and develop sales and marketing personnel.
- To initiate, organize, and attend sales- and marketing-related seminars, conferences, and courses.

Of course, a list like this one cannot begin to communicate the especially creative and dynamic nature of the position we are offering you. As associate director of marketing, you will have a vital and creative role in helping to shape P.J. Guilford policies and objectives, in leading people who work for P.J. Guilford to become more effective in their careers, and in representing P.J. Guilford to other important companies, institutions, and individuals.

I hope you are as excited as we are about your prospects in this position. I am convinced that an outstanding career awaits you at P.J. Guilford. We would like you to begin that career on September 8, but the final starting date is negotiable, according to your needs.

Please let me know your decision about this offer before August 1. I am very much looking forward to a "yes" answer, and if it is, we can begin immediately to discuss your future at P.J. Guilford in more detail.

Sincerely,
(signed first name)
ALFRED GRANT
VP, Marketing

To the vice president of marketing at P.J. Guilford, Inc., from a job applicant expressing unqualified *acceptance of the position of associate director of marketing* (NOTE: *The related job-offer letter appears directly above. In the letter below, the writer greets the recipient informally, by first name, because that practice was established by the recipient in his previous letter. She is also careful simply to "accept" the salary offer rather than to express enthusiasm over it. To do otherwise might imply that the salary offer exceeds what she merits.):*

Dear Alfred,

Your letter of July 20 was a most welcome one. I am happy to accept the position of associate director of marketing at P.J. Guilford, Inc., that you have offered me. The salary of $55,000 is acceptable to me, and so are the benefits and incentive options offered in the Confidential Personnel Memorandum that accompanied your letter.

I am eager to begin my employment on September 8, the day that you suggested. In the meantime I am available for any further discussions you would like to have about my job functions or responsibilities.

As you know, P.J. Guilford, Inc., is an organization I have long admired for its enterprise and its professionalism. I am very proud of becoming a part of it in such an exciting capacity. I look forward to working with you and with everyone else at P.J. Guilford, Inc., to keep it at the very top of its field.

Sincerely,
(signed first name)
RUTH STETSON

To the vice president of marketing at P.J. Guilford, Inc., from a job applicant expressing conditional *acceptance of the position of associate director of marketing* (NOTE: *In this letter the writer greets the applicant informally, by first name, because that practice was established by the recipient. She is also careful not to mention a specific dollar amount when asking for a higher salary, leaving room for negotiation or retreat. The related job-offer letter appears two letters above. Directly above this letter is an unqualified acceptance letter.*):

Dear Alfred,

Thank you for your letter of July 20, offering me the position of associate director of marketing at P.J. Guilford, Inc. I am very proud that P.J. Guilford has chosen me for this important position, and I am eager to work with you and the other fine members of your organization. However, before I can accept your offer, I must ask you to reconsider the annual salary of $55,000.

I believe that the services and commitment I can bring to P.J. Guilford warrant a higher annual salary. It is a measure of my trust and confidence in you that I express my opinion frankly and appeal to you for a revised figure.

Please let me know if there is anything I can do to assist you in renegotiating your offer for this very exciting position. I am prepared to keep myself eligible for immediate employment at P.J. Guilford for the next two weeks, so that we have time to resolve this matter together.

Thanks again for your kind regard and enthusiastic offer. It is my sincere hope that I can ultimately accept the position and justify your good faith.

Sincerely,
(signed first name)
RUTH STETSON

To someone who submitted an article for publication in Millbury Magazine, *from the editor:*

Dear Ms. Sweeney,

Thank you for sending *Millbury Magazine* your article "Race and Religion," which we received on March 6. It is a sensitive and thought-provoking work, and we would very much like to publish it.

After reviewing the enclosed Comment Sheet and Writer's Agreement, please contact me if you have any questions. Otherwise, please sign both copies of both documents and return them to me for final processing at your earliest convenience. I will then add my signature to all copies and send you a set.

As you will see in the Comment Sheet, we are requesting only a few, relatively minor changes in order to enhance the appeal of your article to our readers. As soon as these changes are made, we can send you payment ($200.00) and set up possible publication dates.

It is a joy and an honor to receive such a well-written piece on such a critically important issue. We are grateful to you for submitting "Race and Religion" to us, and we hope it represents just the beginning of a mutually beneficial relationship.

Yours truly,
ANN CORWIN

To a candidate for membership in the Fortnightly Club, from the club president (NOTE: *Strictly speaking, the writer of this letter is announcing to the recipient, who applied for membership, that he has been accepted. However, the writer of this kind of acceptance letter should always "invite" the recipient to become a member, without stating whether the invitation reflects a knowledge of the recipient from some other source, an application on the recipient's part, or a vote by the membership of the club. For a positive response to the following letter, see the letter immediately after it; for a negative response, see "Letters of Rejection."*):

Dear Mr. Breitmeyer:

As president of the Fortnightly Club, I am happy to invite you to become a member. We are an organization of citizens who are committed to advancing humanitarian causes within the community, and we believe that you would enjoy working with us in that endeavor.

I look forward to welcoming you into the Fortnightly Club personally during our next meeting on Friday, September 16, at 8 p.m., at the Atrium Club, 1313 Second Avenue. Please let me know if you will be attending.

Sincerely,
RICHARD WARD
President

To a club president, from a person accepting the president's invitation to join the club (NOTE: *When confirming a date, time, and place in a letter, as the writer below does, always repeat the details so that the recipient can be sure that you have the correct information.):*

Dear Mr. Ward,
   I am very pleased to accept your August 23 invitation to join the Fortnightly Club. Please count on me to attend your next meeting on Friday, September 16, at 8 p.m., at the Atrium Club, 1313 Second Avenue.
   I have long admired the work of the Fortnightly Club, and I'm honored that you consider me worthy to be included in your ranks. For many years, community service has been an important and rewarding part of my life. Being able to share that commitment with people who are talented, resourceful, and well-respected business leaders in Cutler City is a real privilege.
   Thank you for extending this opportunity to me. I'm eager to meet you and the other Fortnightly Club members next month.

Sincerely,
Lewis Breitmeyer

LETTERS OF REJECTION

The best letters of rejection are brief, tactful, and as upbeat as possible without being insensitive or false. In most situations it is wise to avoid mentioning specific reasons for the rejection. Personal reasons (e.g., not liking an applicant's appearance or personality) should never be mentioned, nor should the "more impressive" qualities of the applicant's competition. An exception may be made if knowing the reason may benefit the recipient without making him or her feel inferior (for an example, see the letter to Ms. Mercedo in this section).
   Here are samples of different kinds of rejection letters applying to different situations:

To someone who applied for a job by letter, but was not interviewed or seriously considered, from a personnel director at Seeley, Inc.:

Dear Ms. Boracci,
   Thank you for your January 18 letter inquiring about possible employment at Seeley, Inc. Although your qualifications are impressive, they do not fit with our current needs.

We will retain your application in our records in case an opportunity arises at another time that is suitable to you and to us. Please accept our best wishes for the future.

Sincerely,
MARK CONNACHER
Personnel Director

To a job applicant who was interviewed and had good qualifications, from the owner of Richmond Fields, who chose someone else:

Dear Mr. Schenko,

I regret to inform you that the position at Richmond Fields for which you applied has been filled by someone else. All of us at Richmond Fields were impressed by your background, qualifications, and professional behavior, and I regret very much that we have no other position to offer you.

I will definitely keep your resumé handy, and I will contact you immediately if another position worthy of your skills becomes available. In any event, it was a pleasure meeting you. Please accept my best wishes for securing the type of fulfilling employment that you deserve.

Sincerely,
DANIEL RUPPERT
President

To a job applicant who was interviewed and who clearly did not qualify, from a director of communications at Kylemont Industries (NOTE: In this situation, the writer appropriately states the specific reason for rejection, since it is not personal and the applicant could well derive benefit from knowing it.):

Dear Ms. Mercedo,

Thank you for coming to Kylemont to be interviewed for the position of media coordinator. I am afraid we are unable to offer you the position at this time.

As I mentioned during our meeting, Kylemont is looking for someone who has had at least two years of work in the public relations field. Although you have had an impressively rich variety of media-related job responsibilities in the past, we still believe that public relations experience is essential for this kind of position, which requires extensive interaction with public relations professionals.

If I have in some way misunderstood your work credentials in this respect, please let me know as soon as possible. Otherwise, I encourage you to seek public relations experience. I am confident that it would be an invaluable asset to you, given your remarkable skills and work history.

Very truly yours,
JOSEPH LIOTTA
Director of Communications

To an employee of ACC, Inc., who requested a transfer, from a personnel manager who is rejecting that request:

Dear Mr. Sanders,

I am afraid we cannot grant your July 17 request for a transfer to the East Lexington branch of ACC, Inc. At present, there are no staff positions available at East Lexington that are suitable for your qualifications, and we do not foresee any positions becoming available in the near future.

I am keeping your request in my active file and will notify you if and when a suitable position at East Lexington becomes available. In the event that you no longer wish to be considered for a transfer, please notify me as soon as possible.

We appreciate your interest in pursuing new career challenges within ACC, Inc. If I can assist you in this endeavor in any other way, please do not hesitate to call me.

Sincerely,
ADAM WATSON
Personnel Manager

To the vice president of Rolleco, from an applicant who was offered a position after he had already accepted another position:

Dear Mr. O'Malley,

Thank you for your letter of April 4, offering me a position at Rolleco as transportation manager. I very much appreciate your interest in me, and the fine opportunity this job represents, but I must regretfully decline your offer. Since I last spoke with you, I have assumed the position of manager of shipping and receiving at Rock Mountain Company.

Please accept my gratitude for your consideration. It was a pleasure meeting you.

Sincerely,
MICHAEL JERROD

To the manager of a television station, from someone who has been offered a job but doesn't want it (NOTE: *In this type of situation, nothing is to be gained by going into the specific reasons why the job is being rejected. The writer of this letter is actually waiting for a better offer from some other organization, but she politely—and accurately—states simply that she has chosen to remain in her present position "for the time being."*):

Dear Mrs. Padden,
I was very honored by your February 18th letter offering me the position of assistant station manager at WRRF. However, I must decline your offer. After much thought and discussion with my family, I have decided to remain in my present position for the time being.
Thank you very much for your kindness and consideration.

Sincerely yours,
LEE YAMATO

To a club president, from an invited member who is rejecting an invitation to join (NOTE: *See above, "Letters of Acceptance," for two related letters. In this type of "rejection" situation, it is not necessary to state the reason for the rejection. However, if you wish to do so, it is always better to offer a nonjudgmental excuse, like time constraints, rather than to offer a criticism of the organization. The latter can be accomplished by means of a separate letter of opinion that focuses directly—and exclusively—on a specific issue. See chapter 12, "Letters of Reference, Commendation, and Opinion," for an example of a letter offering constructive criticism.*):

Dear Mr. Ward,
Thank you for your August 23 invitation to join the Fortnightly Club. I regret that I must decline the invitation. At present, my schedule does not allow time for active involvement in your organization.
Please accept my regrets and good wishes.

Sincerely,
LEWIS BREITMEYER

LETTERS OF RESIGNATION

Regardless of the circumstances, a letter of resignation should be brief, formal, and positive in tone. It will be a final and lasting reminder of your affiliation with the organization to which it is addressed, and at all costs, you want it to communicate goodwill, efficiency, and professionalism.

If the situation compelling you to resign is a negative one that occurred within the organization, it won't do any good to discuss it in your letter of resignation. It is better simply to use your letter to announce your intention to resign and to specify (or suggest) your last working day.

Here are additional guidelines:

- Properly speaking, if you are leaving an organization altogether, you should state that you are resigning from that organization, and not from your position within that organization. A writer would say, for example, "Please accept my resignation from the Highmount Citizens Group," instead of "Please accept my resignation as secretary of the Highmount Citizens Group."

  Suppose that the same writer were resigning from the position of secretary rather than from the organization itself. In this case, the letter would say, "Please accept my resignation as secretary of the Highmount Citizens Group. At this time, I prefer to remain in the group as a member, not an officer."

- Although it is not necessary to refer either to your reasons for resigning or to your future plans, you may wish to do so briefly as a courtesy, assuming that your reference will not reflect negatively on the organization you are leaving.

- It is always wise to call brief attention to your length of service, roles, and if appropriate, major accomplishments at the organization you are leaving. This is especially true if you are leaving under adverse circumstances. Your letter will be a final statement validating that you have been an integral and productive member of that organization.

- Whenever possible, express gratitude for the experiences that you've had and the people with whom you've worked at the organization you are leaving. Just be careful to be concise and not overly effusive. Sentimental goodbyes are best made face to face.

Here are examples of different kinds of resignation letters applying to various types of situations:

To a vice president at Mann & Mann, from a manager who is retiring by choice:

Dear Mrs. Gaffney,

Please accept my resignation from Mann & Mann effective July 1, 1995. After 10 years of service with this fine company, it is my wish to retire.

My career at Mann & Mann, beginning as an assistant administrator and progressing to Manager of the Production Department, has brought me a wonderful sense of accomplishment and a great deal of pride. Most of all, however, I am grateful for the close personal and professional relationships I have developed with many of the wonderful people who work here, including you.

I will always remember Mann & Mann and the people at Mann & Mann fondly.

Very truly yours,
MICHAEL SMITH

To the president of Linden Company, from a general manager who is resigning due to a negative and unresolvable work situation (NOTE: *The writer of this letter has an entrenched personality conflict with her new boss, who is the recipient's subordinate and is unable to transfer to another position that is comparable or better. To protect her own dignity and self-interest, she is careful to avoid both bitter allusions or false effusions. Instead, she simply calls attention to her major accomplishment as a Linden employee.*):

Dear Mr. Marsh,

Regretfully, I must ask you to accept my resignation from Linden Company after six years of employment. I would like March 16, 1995, to be my final date of employment.

My experience at Linden Company has taught me a great deal, for which I shall always be grateful. As Linden's General Manager for the past three years, I am especially proud of having reorganized most of the product assembly processes, so that Linden is now 25 percent more efficient than it was two years ago.

Thank you for your attention to this matter. Please feel free to contact me in the future if I can be of service to you or to Linden Company.

Sincerely,
JUDITH HARTWELL

To a Union National Bank vice president, from someone who is retiring due to poor health:

Dear Mr. Nash,

It is with much regret that I submit my resignation from Union National Bank, effective March 31, 1994. My health will not permit me to continue fulfilling my work responsibilities as I would prefer.

My 15-year association with Union National Bank has been a happy and productive one. I shall miss the work and the people very much. Please accept my best wishes for future success.

Sincerely,
FRANK HAGEDORN

To Mount Vernal Community Center's general manager, from an assistant manager who is leaving to accept another job (NOTE: *The writer has a relatively friendly, informal relationship with the recipient and the other staff members.*):

Dear Ms. Blume,

After three enjoyable years at Mount Vernal Community Center, I must now submit my resignation, effective May 1, 1994. I have decided to accept a position offered to me by Energetics Associates.

Mount Vernal Community Center is a fine organization, which has contributed much to my own life and to the lives of all the people who live in Oakdale. It has been an honor and a pleasure to work with you and the rest of the staff. I hope we will continue to stay in touch.

Sincerely,
MELISSA MCCABE

To a club president, from a member who is resigning because she is moving:

Dear Ms. Carlson,

Regretfully, I must submit my resignation from the Friends and Neighbors Club, effective June 30. My husband and I are moving to Minneapolis in July.

I have thoroughly enjoyed my eight years of membership in this outstanding organization, especially the past three years working with the board of officers as treasurer and social chairperson. As soon as I'm settled in my new home, I hope to become involved with a similar organization.

Please accept my very best wishes for a successful future, and never forget that you have a friend and ally in Minnesota.

Sincerely yours,
JUDITH LEVI

PART FOUR

Appendix

Parts of a Letter

THE BASIC PARTS of a social, business, or official letter (not a memorandum) are listed below in the order in which they most commonly appear in a letter: from the beginning (i.e., top of the first or single page) to the end (i.e., bottom of the last or single page). While it is helpful to know what parts a letter is expected to contain, two points are important to keep in mind:

- Not all social or business letters feature all of these parts. A social letter, for example, would probably not include an inside address and may not include a heading, assuming it is very informal. An informal business or official letter may not include any notation elements and may or may not include a subject line, depending on the writer's preference.

- It is perfectly acceptable to customize letter formats to fit your individual needs. For example, you may want to indicate your telephone number in an extra line added to the heading, or you may want to relocate the heading so that it is directly below your printed name at the end of the letter.

  The secret to good taste lies in striking a proper balance between conventional format and personal style. You don't want to stray too far from the conventional format out of respect for your reader; after all, it's the most widely accepted and therefore convenient format to read. However, slight adaptations to that style may better suit individual letters or letter writers.

For more information, see "Standard Correspondence Formats" in this Appendix. On each model letter in the "Standard Correspondence Formats" section, the parts of the letter are indicated by number, as listed below.

1. Heading

This is the writer's full address. With some stationery, a preprinted letterhead constitutes the heading. For informal letters, a heading is optional.

2. Date

This is the month, day, and year when you are writing the letter.

3. Inside address

This is the recipient's full name and address. Informal letters generally do not include an inside address.

4. Subject line

This is a word or phrase indicating the main subject of the letter, usually introduced by the word "Subject:" or "Re:" (Latin for "matter"). It is an optional feature of business or official letters; it is not appropriate for social correspondence.

5. Greeting

Also known as the "salutation," this is the introductory phrase "Dear [name of recipient]." It can end with either a comma or a colon. Today, a comma is more often used, except if only a title, not a proper name, appears, in which case a colon is more appropriate (e.g. "Dear applicant:").

6. Body

This is the complete text of the letter.

7. Closing

This is the farewell word or phrase that precedes the signature; common examples include "Sincerely," "Yours truly," "Best wishes," and "Love." (The latter two greetings are more appropriate for informal correspondence.)

8. Signature

This is the signed name of the writer. In business or formal correspondence, the full name of the writer is printed directly below the signed name, even when the signed name is *not* the full name. A further addition in a business or formal letter may be the recipient's title, which is printed directly below the printed name.

9. Postscript

This is a brief paragraph of additional content, introduced by the initials "P.S." for "post scriptus," Latin for "after having been written." It implies that the reader, having completed and signed the letter, has an afterthought. Although still relatively common in informal, handwritten letters, its use in printed letters is increasingly rare, since it suggests lack of careful planning before composing the letter.

10. Notation elements

This part of a business or formal letter consists of initials, abbreviations, or brief words that offer "coded" information pertaining to the letter. They usually appear in the lower left-hand corner of the last page.

Specific notation elements that might appear in a letter are listed below. If there are multiple notation elements, they should be stacked vertically in the order reflected below.

(a) "Please reply" or "R.s.v.p." ("Répondez s'il vous plaît," French for "Respond, if you please")

This notation element indicates that the recipient is expected to contact the writer with a "yes" or "no" answer to an invitation made in the body of the letter. Often, an address and/or telephone number is printed directly below.

(b) "cc:" or "copy:" or "copies:"

Followed by a name or a column of names, any one of these notation elements indicates people to whom copies of the letter are being sent.

(c) "enc." or "enclosure"

Either of these notations indicates that something else accompanies the letter (e.g., a resumé, a gift, or a report).

(d) "AD/kl"

This notation element applies to situations in which a person printed or even composed a letter on behalf of someone else. The specific initials used here are exemplary rather than standard.

The capitalized initials on the left are those of the author of the letter—i.e., the "I" in the body of the letter (in this case, "Allan Davis"). The lower-case initials on the right are those of the person who literally printed or composed the letter (in this case, "Keith Leonard"). A common situation calling for this type of notation element would be when a secretary actually composed and typed the final version of a letter that was dictated by his or her boss.

Standard Correspondence Formats

THE FOUR standard correspondence formats are described below. They are then illustrated by three sample letters (on which the parts of a letter are number-coded) and one sample memorandum.

1. Block Format

All parts of the letter (with the exception of the heading, assuming there is no letterhead) are flush against the left margin of the page. Paragraphs in the body of the letter begin flush left, with a blank line dividing each paragraph. This format is primarily used in business and official letters, rather than social letters.

2. Semiblock Format

The heading (assuming there is no letterhead), date, and signature are aligned on the right side of the page. All other elements are flush left. Paragraphs in the body of the letter begin flush left, with a blank line dividing each paragraph. This format is appropriate for business and official letters as well as social letters.

3. Indented Format

Assuming there is a letterhead, the date is centered on the page directly below the letterhead. Assuming there is no letterhead, the heading and date are aligned on the right side of the page. The greeting is flush left. Paragraphs in the body of the letter are indented, with no blank line between paragraphs. The signature is on the right-hand side of the page (aligned with the heading and date if there is no letterhead). This format is appropriate for business, official, or social correspondence.

4. Memorandum

This is a business-oriented format that is best used for interoffice or intercolleague correspondence. Preceding the body of the memorandum are four lines stacked flush left: "To:," "From:," "Date:," and "Re:" or "Subject:."

BLOCK FORMAT

① ↙

PTNA
2504 Lancaster Street
Chicago, IL 60632[*]

②→ March 21, 1994

③→ Michael Gennaro
1818 Cremona Circle
Philadelphia, PA 19146

④→ Subject: Keynote Speaker, PTNA Annual Convention

⑤→ Dear Dr. Gennaro,

The Professional Trainers of North America, a
nationwide organization of management trainers,
would be very pleased and honored if you would
speak at our annual convention this June in
Detroit, Michigan. Specifically, we would like you
to deliver the keynote address on opening night,
Friday, June 10, 1994, at 8 p.m. Our theme for this
↗ year is ''Motivating Good Performance.''
⑥
↘ If this is agreeable to you, please let me know your
fees, terms, and equipment needs at your earliest
convenience.

I sincerely hope to have the pleasure of welcoming
you to this year's PTNA convention. Your

---

* On letterhead stationery, there is usually no need to write a heading for the
letter.

participation will make it a very exciting and memorable event for all of us.

⑦→ Very truly yours,

 (signed name)

⑧

 Walter Weaver
 President

⑩→ cc: Annette Colsen, Social Chairperson, PTNA

⑩→ WW/bd

SEMIBLOCK FORMAT

Heaven Hollow Farms←①
RR # 23, Box 411
Dexter, MA 01390[*]

August 10, 1994←②

Marianne Hardiwick
③→ 1803 Wheelersburg Road
Portsmouth, OH 45662

⑤→ Dear Ms. Hardiwick,

Thank you for writing us on August 2 to express your interest in the recipe for Heaven Hollow Cranberry Mustard. We are very proud of this product and pleased that you enjoy it. Unfortunately, we cannot publicly reveal the precise mixture of ingredients that gives our mustard its unique taste.

⑥

Please understand our need to protect our recipes so that we can continue to stay in business and to provide our customers with the very best products of their type available in the marketplace.

Because you were so kind to let us know how much you like Heaven Hollow Cranberry Mustard, I am enclosing a catalog that not only describes our full line of delicious mustards, ketchups, salad dressings, spreads, and dips, but also offers a number of easy and delightful recipes for salads, sandwiches, side dishes, and party food.

Thanks again for writing.

⑦→ Sincerely,

(signed name)

⑧ Dale Logan
Customer Service Manager

⑩→ enclosure

* On letterhead stationery, there is usually no need to write a heading for the letter.

INDENTED FORMAT

43 Apache Lane←①
Fremont, Arizona 86420[*]

June 12, 1994←②

Joseph Weidner
③→ 144 Zuni Street
Fremont, Arizona 86420[**]

⑤→ Dear Mr. Weidner,

⑥

I am writing to let you know how much I appreciate your helping my son Robert last Thursday when he sprained his ankle. It meant a great deal to him to have someone extend comfort and care at such a distressing time.

Robert's ankle is healing well, and he should be his normal, active self again in about a week. He joins the rest of my family in thanking you for your kindness.

Very truly yours,←⑦
(signed name)←⑧

Philip Canoff[***]

* On stationery with a letterhead, the heading is usually not necessary and the date should be centered directly below the letterhead.
** In a more informal version of this letter, the inside address would not be necessary.
*** In a more informal version of this letter, the printed name is not necessary, assuming the signature is easily legible.

MEMORANDUM

To: George Casswell
        Henry Fox
        Lynn Sultana[*]

From: Jerome Lyndon
        President, East-West Products[**]

Date: July 20, 1994

Re: Second Quarter Sales Report[***]

I am pleased to report that East-West Products sold a record $995,000 worth of Paisley Pagodas during the last quarter (April 1 through June 30). You are all to be commended for your help in making this our most successful season ever.

As you know, our goal for this quarter is $110,000. With your good work, I am confident we can reach it![****]

cc: Frances Ngu, Chairperson of the Board

JL/sy

---

* Addressees are usually listed in alphabetical order by last name. If titles are used (e.g., George Casswell, VP, Marketing [one line]), addressees are listed by rank; however, titles are generally not used unless the addressees are unfamiliar with each other.

** The title of the writer, if any, is usually printed directly below the name.

*** The subject line may be emphasized by underlining or using all capital letters.

**** The text may be either indented or block format.

Special Forms of Address

United States Government Officials

PRESIDENT OF THE UNITED STATES
Inside address: The President of the United States
The White House
Greeting: Dear Mr./Madam President

VICE PRESIDENT OF THE UNITED STATES
Inside address: The Vice President of the United States
The White House
Greeting: Dear Mr./Madam Vice President

CHIEF JUSTICE OF THE U.S. SUPREME COURT
Inside address: The Chief Justice of the United States
The Supreme Court of the United States
Greeting: Dear Mr./Madam Chief Justice

ASSOCIATE JUSTICE OF THE SUPREME COURT
Inside address: Justice Kathleen O'Neill
The Supreme Court of the United States
Greeting: Dear Justice O'Neill

CABINET OFFICER
Inside address: The Honorable Donald Richter
Secretary of State
(address of State Department)

Greeting: Dear Mr. Secretary [If a woman, write "Dear Madam Secretary."]

U.S. SENATOR
Inside address (Washington, D.C.): The Honorable Janis Hearndon
United States Senate
(office address)
(Elsewhere): The Honorable Janis Hearndon
United States Senator
(address)
Greeting: Dear Senator Hearndon
(NOTE: The same format applies to state senators.)

U.S. REPRESENTATIVE
Inside address (Washington, D.C.): The Honorable John Finch
House of Representatives
(office address)
(Elsewhere): The Honorable John Finch
Representative in Congress
(address)
Greeting: Dear Mr. Finch
(NOTE: The same format applies to state representatives, assemblypeople, or delegates.)

FORMER PRESIDENT, VICE PRESIDENT, SUPREME COURT JUSTICE, CABINET MEMBER, OR U.S. SENATOR/REPRESENTATIVE
Inside address: The Honorable Dalton Kincaid
(street/city or town/zip code)
Greeting: Dear Mr. Kincaid

U.S. AMBASSADOR
Inside address: The Honorable Malcolm Rudolph
American Ambassador [If not at his or her post, write, for example, "American Ambassador to France."]
(address)
Greeting: Dear Ambassador Rudolph

FOREIGN AMBASSADOR IN THE UNITED STATES
Inside address: His/Her Excellency, Ulant Tooma
          Ambassador of Keenua
          (address)
Greeting: Dear Mr./Madam Ambassador

GOVERNOR OF A STATE OR TERRITORY
Inside address: The Honorable Thomas DeVonne
          Governor of Illinois
Greeting: Dear Governor DeVonne

DISTRICT ATTORNEY
Inside address: The Honorable Maxwell Hammer
          District Attorney, Franklin County
          County Courthouse
          (address)
Greeting: Dear Mr. Hammer

MAYOR
Inside address: The Honorable Dianne Sheppard
          Mayor of Montgomery
          (address)
Greeting: Dear Madam Mayor [If a male, write "Dear Mr. Mayor"]

MILITARY TITLE
Inside address: General Adam Howard, USA
          (address)
   (NOTE: Substitute any title, written out rather than abbreviated, for "General." The designator "USA" means "U.S. Army." Designators for other services are: Navy, "USN"; Air Force, "USAF"; Marine Corps, "USMC"; Coast Guard, "USCG." Reserve status is indicated by adding "R" to the designator, e.g., "USAR" for "U.S. Army Reserves.")
Greeting: Dear General Howard
   (NOTE: Substitute any title for "General," with the exception of the following ranks, for which you should use "Mr./Ms." and the last name: in the Army/Air Force/Marine Corps: Chief Warrant

Office, Warrant Office, Sergeant, Private; in the Navy/Coast Guard: Lieutenant, Lieutenant Junior Grade, Ensign.)

Religious Officials of the Roman Catholic Church

THE POPE
Inside address: His Holiness, Pope John XXIV
Vatican City
(address)
Greeting: Your Holiness

CARDINAL IN THE UNITED STATES
Inside address: His Eminence, John Cardinal Frias
Archbishop of Chicago
(address)
Greeting: Dear Cardinal Frias

ROMAN CATHOLIC ARCHBISHOP/BISHOP IN THE UNITED STATES
Inside address: The Most Reverend Michael E. Payton, D.D.
Archbishop/Bishop of Denver
(address)
Greeting: Dear Archbishop/Bishop Payton

ROMAN CATHOLIC PRIEST
Inside address: The Reverend Martin Schuyler
(address)
Greeting: Dear Father Schuyler [If the priest has a doctor's degree, use "Dear Dr. Schuyler."]

ROMAN CATHOLIC/PROTESTANT MOTHER SUPERIOR
Inside address: The Reverend Mother Superior
Convent of St. Matthew
(address)
Greeting: Dear Mother Superior

ROMAN CATHOLIC SISTER
Inside address: Sister Mary L. Taylor
(address)
Greeting: Dear Sister Taylor

Religious Officials of the Jewish Faith

RABBI
Inside address: Rabbi Myron Nussbaum
　　　　　　　(address)
Greeting: Dear Rabbi Nussbaum

Religious Officials of Protestant Denominations

METHODIST BISHOP
Inside address: The Reverend Lucas Diefenbach
　　　　　　　Methodist Bishop
　　　　　　　(address)
Greeting: Dear Bishop Diefenbach

EPISCOPAL BISHOP
Inside address: The Right Reverend Kenneth Ewing
　　　　　　　Bishop of Miami
　　　　　　　(address)
Greeting: Dear Bishop Ewing

ARCHDEACON
Inside address: The Venerable Stephen Mays
　　　　　　　Archdeacon of Omaha
　　　　　　　(address)
Greeting: Dear Archdeacon

CANON
Inside address: The Reverend William Gleason
　　　　　　　Canon of St. George's
　　　　　　　(address)
Greeting: Dear Canon Gleason

EPISCOPAL PRIEST
Inside address: The Reverend Martin Schuyler
　　　　　　　(address)
Greeting: Dear Father Schuyler

MINISTER

Inside address: The Reverend Alice Latour
               (address)

Greeting: Dear Ms. Latour [If the minister has a doctor's degree, "Dear Dr. Latour."]

Index

JACK MAGUIRE is the author of 22 books specializing in the fields of communication, business, education, and personal development. He also writes and produces instructional and educational video courses, including *Effective Writing for Executives, Writing at Work,* and *Effective Communication* for Time Life Video. As an assistant professor, he taught composition, language, and business communication courses at Memphis State University and at Shelby State University (both in Memphis, Tennessee). He lives in Highland, New York.

Among the books authored:

500 Terrific Ideas for Home Maintenance
Kids' Rooms
Outdoor Spaces
Spas and Hot Tubs, Saunas and Home Gyms
Creative Storytelling: Choosing, Inventing, & Sharing
  Tales for Children
Night & Day: Use the Power of Your Dreams to Transform Your Life
Who's Stealing Your Business: How to Identify & Prevent Business
  Espionage